PET ROCKS® • RENT-A-WRECK® •
FRISBEE® • CELESTIAL SEASONINGS®—

these are just a few of the extraordinary, real-life successes
you will discover within these pages. Each of these stories
is as sharply individual as the people who dared to chart
their own paths to the top and had the ingenuity and true
grit to reach and surpass their goals. A very few of them
had enough money to back their own innovative ideas. But
most of them had to come up with ingenious methods to
get even the small amount of capital they began with. What
all of these stories offer is the very special human interest,
rich inspiration, and invaluable lessons that only success
can provide. If you want to get a true idea of how to make
it big in America today with just your own originality and
determination, here is the book that can show you the way.

WHY DIDN'T I THINK OF THAT!

"Great stories . . . lasting curiosity value."

—*Kirkus Reviews*

SIGNET Titles for Your Reference Shelf

WHY DIDN'T I THINK OF THAT!

by Robert L. Shook

A SIGNET BOOK

NEW AMERICAN LIBRARY

TIMES MIRROR

PUBLISHED BY
THE NEW AMERICAN LIBRARY
OF CANADA LIMITED

Pet Rock® is the registered trademark of Rock Bottom Productions.
Slinky® is the registered trademark of James Industries Inc.
The Hula Hoop® Toy, The Frisbee® Disc, and The Super Ball®
    Toy are the registered trademarks of Wham-O Mfg. Co.
The Erotic Baker® is the registered trademark of the Erotic
    Baker, Inc.
Eastern Onion™ is the registered trademark of Eastern Onion, Inc.
Rent-A-Wreck® is the registered trademark of Rent-A-Wreck,
    a division of Bundy American Corporation.
BabyLand General™ is the registered trademark of Original
    Appalachian Artworks, Inc. DBA Babyland General.
Toughman Contest™ is the registered trademark of Ardore Ltd.
Celestial Seasonings® is the registered trademark of Celestial
    Seasonings, Inc.

First Printing, June, 1983

2   3   4   5   6   7   8   9

 SIGNET TRADEMARK REG. U.S. PAT. OFF. AND FOREIGN COUNTRIES
REGISTERED TRADEMARK - MARCA REGISTRADA
HECHO EN WINNIPEG, CANADA

SIGNET, SIGNET CLASSICS, MENTOR, PLUME, MERIDIAN
and NAL BOOKS are published in Canada by The New American
Library of Canada, Limited, Scarborough, Ontario

PRINTED IN CANADA
COVER PRINTED IN U.S.A.

Acknowledgments

Several people were particularly helpful in the research and preparation of this manuscript. I would like to acknowledge my gratitude to LaVina Abbott, Linda J. Allen, Gary Cheses, Victoria Danis, Jeanne Desy, Joe Goldring, Mark S. Grody, Goldy Norton, Joan Sanger, Reed Trencher, Sherry Wier, and Al Zuckerman.

**To my son, Michael,
who always asks why**

Contents

Introduction

"Every new opinion, at its starting, is precisely in a minority of one."

Thomas Carlyle

A Pet Rock? A Hula Hoop? A Mood ring? If you're like most people, your first reaction to such a product is: "Why didn't I think of it first?" In fact, chances are that at some time during your life you have thought up some equally unusual product or service—only to discard the possibility because somebody told you it wouldn't work.

However, don't despair. An irate banker once demanded that Alexander Graham Bell remove "that toy" from his office. To the banker, the world's first telephone was a dumb idea.

It should come as no surprise that just about every entrepreneur in this book heard the same thing from family and friends: "Forget it. It's a dumb idea." They refused to forget it, and time has shown that the ideas were not so dumb after all—in fact, they were brilliant. But more important, these people *believed* in their ideas, and stuck with them even when the going got rough. They were enthusiastic and tenacious; they refused to fail.

As somebody once said, "Ideas are a dime a dozen—but the men and women who can implement them are priceless." When the idea is an *X*-rated bakery or a *used*-car rental service, the problems are endless—the ability to overcome the obstacles and keep moving forward is what counts. It takes a very special kind of person to figure out how to promote a unique product or service and develop a one-of-a-kind business.

Of course, good timing helps, and it's nice to be blessed with some good luck. A number of the people in this book testify to a few lucky breaks along the way. On the other hand, they were smart enough to take advantage of good luck when it came their way. In listening to their stories, you can't help but think that they would have kept on believing and working until somehow or other they did "get lucky."

The fact is that a lot of "brilliant ideas" bite the dust. Why did these ideas succeed? Hard work, luck, enthusiasm—and some know-how. Most of these entrepreneurs learned how to overcome obstacles by trial and error; they learned by doing. The businesses had to be financed, for instance; sometimes that seemed like an insurmountable problem. But when Dave Schwartz couldn't find anyone to capitalize his used-car rental business, he figured out a way to do it without capital. And when Mary Flatt realized that the only way to capitalize Eastern Onion singing telegrams was to sell her car, she did it. Promoting an idea without cash can also look impossible—but Gary Dahl got a million dollars' worth of publicity for his Pet Rock and never spent a penny on advertising.

The ten stories in this book are the stories of ordinary people who attained the American Dream. Each of them is self-made; almost none of them had much experience in running a business. Several did not complete college, and none had a sophisticated business education.

These stories also demonstrate how fickle the American public often is. For instance, the Pet Rock and the Mood ring were overnight successes that racked up millions of dollars in sales and died as suddenly as they had started. The Hula Hoop fad also faded away, but several years later the product made a remarkable comeback. Other products like the Frisbee and Slinky have withstood the test of time and are now being enjoyed by a second generation of Americans. It's interesting to note, however, that the Frisbee was very slow to become popular, and was not widely accepted until several years after it was introduced.

While the Slinky, the Frisbee, and the other products and services in this book are patented, nobody has a patent on success. The stories in *Why Didn't I Think of That!* show how these ten ordinary people did it in the face of obstacles and discouragement. Though their ideas cannot be copied, their ingenuity and persistence can. In fact, you may be the one to do it. And when you've made your millions on a bright (or "dumb") idea, you too can have the satisfaction of hearing people say, "Why didn't *I* think of that!"

amid the Shiny, the Tubes, and the other noodles, and
so-forth in this book are entire... in...ch. The most of it rest.
The stories in Whamdex! (Tales of?) Tech show how... as
...characters point out in the face of... disasters and discovery
plant. To split their trees cannot be cored, their insanity and
why patrons... In fact, you... the compelled to it. And other
planets would it cause on a couple of earth... I [take] you
too can have the population of reading people... Why don't
I think of that.

The Pet Rock®

The multimillion-dollar Pet Rock fad of late 1975 was probably the most outrageous craze in American history. Gary Dahl's humorous product took the country by storm, as people from every walk of life rushed out to buy lovable oval rocks at four dollars apiece. At the height of the fad, CBS showed footage of two women shoppers at Bloomingdale's arguing over who saw one particular Pet Rock first. "Apparently," said the straight-faced commentator, "some rocks make better pets than others."

"They were all genuine, pedigreed Pet Rocks, though," Gary Dahl insists, tossing back his leonine head and laughing. The creator of the Pet Rock is dressed nautically today, in white pants and a casual shirt; on other occasions he's western, in Levi's and cowboy boots. The neat full auburn beard completes either look, and the sense of humor that started the whole thing is evident in his light-blue eyes. An easygoing, affable talker, Gary Dahl today has the look of a man who doesn't have a single worry in the world.

However, life before the Pet Rock wasn't always so sweet for Gary as it is now. After spending fifteen years in advertising as a commercial artist and copywriter attempting to work his way up to creative director of a medium-size agency, he decided to quit his thirty-thousand-dollar-a-year job.

"After working on twenty different creative projects a day"—

he sighs—"I felt as though I had burned myself out." Marguerite (now Gary's wife), who was earning some money as a substitute schoolteacher and part-time cocktail waitress, encouraged him to quit and go into free-lance copywriting.

"What she said," Gary says with a wry expression, "was that I should just quit the damn job before I had my heart attack or got an ulcer. And I did. Went in the next day and quit. This was in mid-1974, when it was fashionable to 'drop out'—hell, everyone was doing it. So the day after Marguerite and I discussed it, I just quit."

At the time the couple lived in a tiny rented cottage in the mountains outside of Los Gatos. Surrounded by redwoods, two dogs, a small pack of cats, and some domesticated goats, the couple made do on Marguerite's income and what Gary earned from occasional copywriting jobs.

Several months passed by, and Gary had grown accustomed to the slow pace of his semiretired state. Then one day he joined some cronies in a daytime drinking bout at the Grog and Sirloin in Los Gatos where Marguerite worked. The casual conversation got around to pets, with everyone complaining about the expense and bother they create. That was when Gary said, "I don't have any problems with my pet." And when all eyes were turned to him, he nonchalantly commented, "I have a pet rock."

The line got quite a laugh and began a conversational game of one-liners. "It blossomed into an all-afternoon affair," Gary says, chuckling, "about all the benefits of owning a pet rock. 'You could tell it to sit, and it would sit forever.' Or someone would say, 'Plays dead like a real pro.' 'Look what you save on food.' And of course, 'There's nothing to training it how to attack.' "

As more drinks were ordered and the joking continued, Gary thought about the reaction his casual comment had created. "If it's getting this kind of enthusiasm from this jaded crowd, there's got to be something there." That evening he turned the idea over in his head, determined to find a way to make money from it. His thoughts were still on the Grog and Sirloin conversation when he retired that evening. "I tossed and turned all night," he remembers. "I couldn't get it out of my head."

The following morning Gary woke up with an idea on how to

use the pet-rock concept. He located an old German shepherd training manual among his books and spent several hours at his typewriter writing a spoof on training a pet rock. The copy used the same format as the typical dog book, going through basic obedience tricks, care and feeding, illness, the whole works. Gary is appalled to remember now that his intention was to write a paperback book that might be sold at a gag shop. "Then I stopped to think, 'My God, if I go out on the shelf with a book, what chance will it have, competing with a million other titles? A life span of maybe a couple of weeks. There just has to be a better way. . . .'

"Then"—Gary leans back and grins broadly—"it dawned on me. Why don't I put a real rock in a box, add a little booklet, and come up with a better way? If I put together quality packaging and quality writing, I could elevate the gag to a higher level than the chattering teeth and plastic dog poop sold in novelty stores. I could have it sold over the counter at gift stores and good department stores."

Once Gary had the idea, he knew beyond a doubt he would go ahead with it. His first move was to contact an old friend, Pat Welch, who worked as an artist for an advertising agency. The pair had a similar sense of humor and had worked together on projects before, with Gary writing copy and Pat doing the art. "I figured Pat was just crazy enough to understand the concept I had," Gary says with a smile.

Gary had no money—a fact he refused to worry about at this point—so he asked Pat to design the packaging in return for 10 percent of the profits. Pat, who did not quite share Gary's enthusiasm, did think the idea had possibilities, and agreed to do it.

"He probably put in a total of thirty or forty hours," Gary guesses. "It took him two weeks to do it. And in those two weeks he created what became a classic in packaging, the Pet Rock box, with its carrying handle and the holes cut in it so the little thing could breathe. He created a *tremendous* look that was immediately identifiable."

Between them, the two men scraped up enough money to pay for typesetting the booklet and package so they were ready to print. Then the problems began to emerge. First of all, price checks revealed the expense both of four-color printing and of manufacturing the little boxes. Beyond that, Gary did not know how he was going to have the product distributed nationally (it did not occur to him to settle for local distribution). While he didn't come into the business cold, like the average inventor, Gary, as he says, "knew how to market a product, but I had no expertise in distribution."

Gary then approached a friend, Harry Hambley, who was in the gift-item business, for advice. Harry, who had sales representatives covering the United States, told Gary the product should be distributed through manufacturing representatives who might add it to the lines they already carried. Taking the advice, Gary made an appointment with a San Francisco representative.

Now he faced the problem of making prototypes of the product. He couldn't afford a die to cut the boxes, and he couldn't afford four-color process. Finally he had a hundred boxes printed in black only. Laboriously he and Pat cut each box by hand, pasted on color Xeroxes, hand-folded and glued the boxes, and packed each one with straw. (Due to Department of Agriculture regulations, the straw was changed to excelsior for shipping the actual product over state lines.)

"Well," Gary says, "by the time we hand-made twelve of them, we were so bored with it that we figured, 'If we can't sell 'em off a dozen, we can't sell 'em.' Remember, at this point we had no idea what to expect. We were still betting blue sky."

Gary claims that Marguerite was supportive. She laughs in rebuttal. A tall, statuesque woman with long bright-red hair, she replies softly, "I thought he was going off his *rocker*. I remember when we would take long walks on the beach in Santa Cruz, and all he'd do was look for the right kind of rock. After a while he even had me doing it. I'd find one and say, 'Is this it?' See, he was looking for a rock with a certain look to it, a kind of perfectly round beach pebble. He was possessed with it. After a while, I was getting bored with it. The whole thing was craziness to me."

"But you humored me," Gary says. He admits, however, that Marguerite did not have much faith in the product. It has now become a standing joke that if Marguerite says a new idea looks lousy, that means it will be a great success.

"Truthfully," Gary adds, "she never said it was *lousy*."

Before even one rock sold, however, Gary did have negative input—from his drinking buddies, some of whom were resentful when they heard his plans. "Heck," he says, "each of them had an equal chance to go ahead and do something with this idea. Had they been willing to put in the incredible time and effort that I did, they certainly could have done it. I remember one of them saying to me, 'You're not *really* going to try to use an idea we talked about at the Grog and Sirloin!' It was as though that was hallowed ground—whatever's talked about in here does not go out in the street!

"I said, 'Hell, yes, and I'm going to make a success of it if I possibly can!' "

It had taken Gary from April to August to get the prototype Pet Rocks ready. His original Rock Training Manual was now reduced from eighty-five pages to a slick thirty-two-page miniature booklet less than three by four inches, which would be packed in each carton. Its cover read in bold print: "CONGRATULATIONS! You are now the owner of a genuine, pedigreed PET ROCK."

At the bottom of the page, the word IMPORTANT leapt out. "Do not remove your Pet Rock from its box before reading Item 1 in this booklet." Item 1 gives you the flavor of the booklet:

> Item 1.
>
> Your new rock is a very sensitive pet and may be slightly traumatized from all the handling and shipping required in bringing the two of you together. While you may look in on your new pet from time to time, it is essential that you leave your rock in its box for a few days. It is advised that you set the box in an area of your home that is to become your PET ROCK's "special place." Some PET ROCK owners have found that the ticking of an alarm clock placed near the box has a soothing effect; especially at night.

It takes most PET ROCKS exactly
three days to acclimate themselves
to their new surroundings. After
seventy-two hours have passed
you may remove the rock from its
box and begin enjoying your new
pet.

Gary took his prototypes to the appointment with the San
Francisco gift representative just in time for the upcoming gift
show. The representative's first reaction was cautious: "You
might have something here, and then maybe you don't."

"He'd never seen anything like it," Gary says with an expan-
sive gesture. "The funniest item he'd ever seen was probably a
pot holder shaped like a frog. But *I* knew it was clever. I believed
in my own sense of humor. I also knew Pat's artwork was super.
What I didn't know was whether or not the Pet Rock could make
any money."

After some persuasion, the representative finally agreed to try
out the item, largely because it wouldn't take up that much
space. "What he said"—Gary enjoys the recollection—"was,
'Well . . . we might sell some.' "

Experienced advertising men, Gary and Pat decided to help
the item sell by making a point-of-purchase display. Almost overnight they came up with a poster that perfectly captured the
whimsy of the Pet Rock. The headline was simple: THEY'RE HERE
—PET ROCKS! The five-foot poster, painted in four colors,
showed six copies of the same photograph of a rock, each with
a different caption under it—Pet Rock Sitting Down; Pet Rock
Standing Up; Pet Rock Playing Dead; and so on. The poster
went in front of the display of the twelve prototype Pet Rocks.

Gary and Pat could not stay away from the show, the first test
of the Rock's appeal. "We lurked around," Gary says, "watching
people's reactions. They'd walk in, see the poster, go over and
pick up a box, and then they'd start reading the book, and they
were just laughing their butts off! It was great! We knew. 'By
God, we've done it!' And we'd find the nearest bar and celebrate."

Although the San Francisco gift show is small compared to the

New York and Los Angeles shows, orders for three thousand Pet Rocks were taken. The price tag to retailers was two dollars, and the Rocks would be marked up to four dollars. Most of the orders were small, obviously test orders from buyers who were willing to take a chance on a case of two dozen at forty-eight dollars wholesale. For a new product, the Rock had done very well. The gift representative told Gary to send it to a friend with a show-room in New York City.

Since the New York gift show had already started, the proto-types were shipped express. The San Francisco representative was now enthusiastic, but his New York contact did not share that feeling and took the Rocks only as a friendly gesture. In the few days remaining in the show, however, he took orders for two thousand more Pet Rocks. Next the Rocks went to a representa-tive in Dallas, who sold another two thousand. Now Gary was positive they would sell. He set a target—a hundred thousand Rocks by Christmas. But he faced a major hurdle: there was still no product. While thousands of Rocks had been ordered, with a shipping date of October 1, there were still only twelve Pet Rocks in existence, the prototypes now moving from show to show. The problem of capitalizing the production finally had to be faced.

The question was: how to come up with the money? "I was tapped out," Gary says with a shrug. None of his relatives had the kind of money it would take, either. One possibility was the owner of the Grog and Sirloin, who had followed the idea with paternal interest all along and claimed to have the capital needed. When he had visited the San Francisco show and seen the buyers' reactions, the owner had become a believer; but he also told Gary, "This thing looks like it's going to be big. Frankly, I don't have the kind of money it's going to take. I've got to back off."

"So now I've got seven thousand units sold, and my angel has disappeared!" Gary laments. "I had to go walking the streets for money. Well, I tried the banks. Can you imagine borrowing money from a bank for a Pet Rock? They didn't exactly tell me I had rocks in my head, but they weren't *about* to lend me the money. Let's say they were polite. Maybe tolerant is a better word. They simply didn't understand it. Banks still don't understand novelty items. I don't think I could borrow from a bank to finance an item even to this day."

After that, Gary called everyone he knew, in town and out of town. What he wanted was $10,000 then, with a possible need for another $50,000 later if the project became successful. No one was willing to take the risk.

Finally he went back to the advertising agency he had worked for and laid out a cost projection for the people there. The first ten thousand units would be expensive, with heavy costs for setting up the printing, which would become cheaper with volume. It worked out to about $10,000. The owner of the agency agreed to give Gary a line of credit at the printers, in return for a percentage of his profits.

The next hurdle was assembly. Gary met with numerous sources, finally settling on the Hope Rehabilitation Center for Physically and Mentally Handicapped, which bid twelve cents a unit. That included packaging, putting twenty-four boxes in a case, and taping the case. "By no means was I being charitable," Gary says. "Hope won the contract on a bid basis."

Just at this point, when the product was financed but Gary personally was out of money, another advertising agency offered him a job as creative director. "I grabbed it," he says with an expressive gesture. "I really needed the dough. Well, I couldn't give the job my best effort, I was so preoccupied with the Pet Rock. I had to quit after three months."

During his time at the agency, one of Gary's preoccupations was finding an appropriate name for his company. In view of the product and his circumstances, he decided on Rock Bottom Productions. In the months to come, many a buyer relaxed and laughed upon placing a frantic call to Gary and hearing a friendly voice answer, "Good morning, you just reached Rock Bottom."

Gary's search for the perfect rock finally took him to a local company that sold rocks wholesale for landscaping purposes. After searching through the samples, he found Rosarita Beach pebbles, imported from Baja, California—nicely rounded rocks, graded for size and measuring about two inches in diameter. "The big joke," the auburn-haired entrepreneur says, "is that the actual rocks only cost about a penny each. By the way, do you need any rocks? I overbought."

While the upfront expenses were high, the total hard cost of goods for the Pet Rock was only 13.5 cents: 1 cent for the rock, 4 cents for the box, 6.5 cents for packaging, and 2 cents for excelsior. By the time Gary paid all his bills, including overhead, assembling expenses, commissions to sales representatives, and a percentage of profits to the advertising agency and to Pat Welch, he realized a gross profit of $1.05 per unit. "That was my target," he explains. "I priced it backwards because I wanted to make a buck per Rock. It would probably have sold just as well at five dollars retail, but who's greedy? I figured four dollars retail was a good price."

On October 5, 1975, with ten people working on an assembly line at the Hope workshop, the first Pet Rocks were shipped out. Gary had missed his October 1 deadline by only four days.

Once the Rocks were in production, he turned his attention to publicity. Since he had no money for advertising, he prepared news releases with a photo of himself surrounded by boxes of Pet Rocks. Marguerite, who was still not convinced Gary's idea would be profitable, approved of the photograph. "He had a great big smile on his face," she recalls, "like a Cheshire cat. It was as if he was saying, 'I'm going to put one over on the public.'"

Optimistically, Gary sent the release to major media. *Newsweek* picked the story up and sent a reporter and photographer to Los Gatos to do a half-page story on Gary and the Pet Rocks. The story included the fact that Neiman-Marcus had just then purchased four dozen Pet Rocks. "And the whole thing exploded!" Gary says. Retailers who read the story decided to follow the lead of Neiman-Marcus. And other major media followed *Newsweek*'s lead. By November 1, all ten thousand Pet Rocks were gone. With media interest increasing every day, Gary decided to go ahead with fifty thousand more units. Before the printing was off the press, those units had been sold.

At this point Gary and the advertising agency had what Gary calls "a slight cash-flow problem." Although the product was selling fast, Rock Bottom had to wait to be paid. In the meantime, the company was also producing more rocks. "We did keep some people waiting a little for their money," Gary admits. "Yeah, we told a few 'Your check is in the mail' lies. But we paid our bills as promptly as could be expected." One thing in Gary's favor was that the stores were reordering fast, which meant prompt payment on the initial orders. Typically, a store that ordered a case of Pet Rocks would sell them all in a day. Neiman-Marcus sold out its four dozen immediately and reordered ten more cases. When those sold in one day, the store ordered fifty more cases. "They went fast," Gary says. "One lady came in and bought ten cases in one purchase!"

Because Rock Bottom was rushing to fill orders, more than one clerical error was made. One department store sent a purchase order for thirty cases; Rock Bottom shipped three hundred. Gary chuckles at the recollection. "This guy was frantic. He called me and screamed, 'Jesus Christ, I just got three hundred cases. Look at my purchase order—I only ordered thirty!' "

With a confident grin Gary says, "I told him, 'Keep 'em. You'll sell 'em. You'll see.' And do you know what? He did sell every single one."

The snowballing publicity on the Pet Rock was helped by department stores, which decided to cash in on the public interest. John Gesicke, the Neiman-Marcus buyer, was one of the first to pose on a street corner with a Pet Rock on a leash. The photograph was picked up by the Dallas newspapers. Gary, well familiar with business wires, also sent out news releases through them to media across the nation. Soon he was being contacted by hundreds of magazines, newspapers, and radio and television stations from all over the country. Everybody wanted to write about the Pet Rock. It had become perhaps the biggest publicity blitz in the history of American business.

Gary was so much in demand that he once gave simultaneous telephone interviews to two radio stations. He appeared on such national television shows as *The Tonight Show* and *Tomorrow*. Since publicity like this cannot be purchased, it is impossible to put a price tag on its value—but an equivalent advertising blitz would have cost many millions. After the craze had ended, Gary was invited to address a marketing group in Los Angeles. "I told them I was very proud of the fact that I never spent a penny to advertise the Pet Rock," he says with a grin. "When they heard that, they died laughing."

This unparalleled media blitz has given the Pet Rock an enduring claim to fame. Gary's success is now studied in marketing classes all over the country as a textbook example of how to launch a product. "You could have fooled me," he says. "I was just following my instincts and doing what I knew how to do. It was not very well plotted out. *Newsweek* picked it up because they'd never seen anything like it. That was luck. It was really good timing."

As the publicity increased, Gary revised his objectives. Realizing the craze might die after Christmas, he decided to try to sell a million units before the holidays. "And by mid-October I knew I could do it," he says. "By God, I wanted to become a millionaire by Christmas!"

When he wasn't juggling media appearances, Gary was working to speed up operations. Rock Bottom had begun with Marguerite doing the typing and invoicing and completing the labels, while Gary did everything from sticking on labels at the warehouse to calling the freight company. "A real Mom and Pop operation," he says, shaking his head. "Well, at its peak we had thirty women typing invoices as fast as they could type!" Production at the Hope workshop accelerated until over three hundred men and women were working on the Pet Rock assembly line.

"It happened so fast we didn't know what hit us," Gary recalls. "We were still living in the little house in the redwoods. One day Marguerite and I went down to the mailbox, which was one of those big rural-route boxes—and it was full, I mean it was *stuffed* with checks. We had checks from Bloomingdale's, Neiman-Marcus, the May Company, Macy's, Lord and Taylor, everyone. There was two hundred thousand dollars in that mailbox.

"We took the mail back to the house and dumped it on the floor and started to go through it. That's when Marguerite became a believer. She looked at me and said, 'You know, Gary, I think this idea is going to work.' God, those were incredible times!"

In mid-November Gary finally had to move operations out of

their five-hundred-square-foot house and into the offices of the advertising agency. He was now working twenty-hour days, seven days a week. Far from being tense and pressured, he found it exhilarating. "The adrenaline was pumping so fast I couldn't stop," he says. "There was no way I could get tired. It was great!

"There were times when I had to ask myself, 'Is this really happening?' I mean, when I'd see those numbers, I just couldn't believe it!" At the peak of the craze, Gary was selling over 100,000 Pet Rocks a day. With over four million dollars in retail sales in a three-month period, the product became one of the most successful gift items in the history of retailing.

Because of the Pet Rock's unforeseen success, Pat Welch's profit had grown to many times more than he had ever expected for his two weeks of part-time work on the package. Gary finally asked him, "Pat, if I write you out a check for fifty grand right now, would you be happy?"

Pat said, "Hell, yes," and Gary gave him a check. It was an amiable solution to a peculiar problem posed by success, and the two men are still good friends today. The advertising agency which originally invested ten thousand dollars plus a credit line in Gary's Pet Rock fared well too, receiving in excess of three hundred thousand by the time the fad was over.

They were prosperous times for Gary and those who shared his faith in the Pet Rock. One of his favorite stories is about the time he and the owner of the advertising agency decided to buy cars.

"With all those big checks coming in the mail, I was feeling really rich," he recalls. "So I thought I should be driving something better than my Honda Civic. We'd been out to lunch, and I'd been in the warehouse that morning, so I had on jeans. I was looking kind of grubby. Well, we walked into a Mercedes-Benz showroom, and I'm sure I looked like I couldn't afford to even look at a Mercedes, let alone buy one. But that was what I wanted. The guy with me wanted one too, and he wanted to buy one for the president of his ad agency.

"So we talked to the salesman and picked out what we wanted, and the whole tab came to around ninety-five grand. The salesman asked, 'How are you going to pay for these?'

"I gestured to the guy with me and said, 'I'll get these, you got lunch.' And I wrote out a check for three Mercedes right there on the spot."

The success of Gary's idea made other luxuries possible. He was able to take a portion of his profits and invest them in a lifelong dream—"one of the finest saloons in northern California," he says with satisfaction.

"My mother had always been in the business," he explains, "so I grew up with this desire to someday own a saloon. I studied this business in college." Gary hired the finest craftsmen available to rebuild the dilapidated bar he bought, and in November 1976 opened Carry Nation's in Los Gatos, a showplace of fine carpentry and leaded glass. The bar, named after the famous Temperance crusader, was another example of Gary's sense of humor and outstanding ability to package a product. "I enjoyed running it for a couple of years," he says, "but it got old. It wasn't what I wanted to do for the rest of my life." When an offer to buy was made, Gary decided to "save my liver and my marriage," and made a good profit on his investment.

Marguerite and Gary realized another lifelong dream in purchasing a thirty-three-foot sloop. Gary points out that he learned a hard lesson with that. "We got so enthused about sailing that I ended up buying the brokerage firm that sold us the boat, along with some waterfront property in Santa Cruz. The problem was that we never got to sail because running the business took all our time!" After eight months the Dahls sold that business for a tidy profit.

In another business venture, Gary brought out The Sand Breeding Kit in 1976—a spoof on the career-change ads that appear on the back of matchbooks and offer to instruct people in everything from motel management to long-haul truck driving in the privacy of their own homes. "If I had come out with it *before* the Pet Rock," Gary says, "I think it would have done as well as the Pet Rock. Personally, I think its writing was superior. But the Pet Rock was so successful that when it died it killed the novelty business—even for me." The stores ordered The Sand Breeding Kits on the basis of Gary's reputation, and seventy thousand units were sold. But the public didn't buy, and there were no reorders.

The Pet Rock also made it possible for the Dahls to buy a Spanish-style white-stucco house ten times larger than the little home in which the business began. Gary delights in pointing out that the swimming pool of the new house is larger than the entire old house. The Dahls are happy with their new home, with its red-tile roof, lavish landscaping, and studio apartment, which Gary uses as a study—with one exception. "We had to get rid of the goats," Marguerite complains, "with all this landscaping. They ate my orchids, too. But it broke my heart to part with them."

The reaction of friends to Gary's success has been a more serious disappointment. In the sleepy little community of Los Gatos (located about sixty miles south of San Francisco), Gary and Marguerite belonged to a group of "good-time people," college-educated dropouts like Gary. "There was a special feeling in that group," Marguerite says sadly. "We were all struggling along. I know things would be different now, 'cause they've all gone back to work. But the fact is, some of them simply stopped being our friends when we became successful."

Gary has become accustomed to the idea that certain people automatically resent a successful man. "Recently my twenty-two-year-old daughter Chris was in a bar," he says, "and a really obnoxious guy said to her, 'I think it's lousy how your dad came to this little town with all his money and threw his weight around.' " Gary throws up his hands in an eloquent gesture. "Now here's a jerk who doesn't know that one day I was poor. I made my money while I was *in* Los Gatos. Hell, I don't even know what that's supposed to *mean*, 'throwing my weight around.' "

Gary has come to distrust the opinions of friends on his ideas. "That's the worst way to do market research," he says emphatically. "Half the time they resent the fact that you want to succeed. They give you negative feedback, and it's the last thing you need when you're excited about a new idea." Despite lack of support from some of his friends, Gary's own faith in himself never wavered. "In the back of my mind I was always convinced I'd eventually make a lot of money," he says thoughtfully. "Like that line from the movie *Patton*, when General Patton says,

'I am destined to do something great.' Well, that's how I always felt."

After the success of the Pet Rock, Gary was sought after by a stream of inventors who wanted his help and advice. In response, he formed a company called Project 80, to provide design, research and development, and marketing services to inventors, manufacturers, and dreamers. "So many people approached me," he explains, "that I figured I might as well be in the business. I wanted to offer an alternative for the person with an idea and no place to go but these so-called invention-development companies. They're nothing but rip-offs. They charge a fee up front with no intention of ever really doing anything. Oh, some of them do a patent search, which anyone can do at the library. Then they charge a few thousand for nothing but promises."

In his work with Project 80, Gary saw thousands of people who lacked the confidence and drive to make an idea work. "I suppose there's a spark in a successful person that separates him from most other people," Gary muses. "I've had so many people approach me with their ideas—they've come to me, mind you —but they're still reluctant to talk about it. They sit across the desk from me, very embarrassed, and slowly pull their little ideas out of their little bags, with a sheepish look on their faces. They're afraid I'm going to laugh at them."

Today Gary no longer operates Project 80, preferring, instead, to develop his own ideas through Gary Dahl Productions, but he still enjoys talking about the concepts that have been brought to him during the past few years. "People used to camp on my doorstep with crazy ideas," he says, laughing. "One guy wanted to come from Louisiana to show me pet elephant dung. I told him to save his money and just send it. Told him I'd call him if I liked it. Another guy—if you can believe this—wanted to sell a crucifixion kit."

As soon as the Pet Rock craze hit, people began to come out with equally inventive follow-up items. There were Pet Rock T-shirts, Pet Rock houses, tiny Pet Rock waterbeds, Pet Rock cars, and even a Pet Rock cemetery. "I didn't create a product," Gary says, "I created a phenomenon. Do you know there was a Pet Rock Obedience Trial Show in Marysville, California—like they have for dogs? I was invited to be grand marshal of this thing. They had a parade and a little Pet Rock orchestra—all these rocks sitting on chairs with music stands. I was blown away!"

Everybody wanted to get on the Pet Rock bandwagon, including people who wished they'd invented the product. Some believed they actually had. One man called on Gary with a gun. He explained to the receptionist that he had thought up the idea several years ago. "Tell Mr. Dahl," he said, waving the pistol, "that I want half of everything he's made on the Pet Rock—or I'm gonna use this! And I know how!" When Gary nervously went to the police, they told him all they could do was put him down as a potential victim. Fortunately, the man with the gun never came back.

A woman from Garden Grove, California, called Gary to inform him that *she* had helped him think of the idea, because she had been sitting in the bar with him and his friends when the famous Pet Rock conversation took place. The only problem was that she insisted the bar was not in Los Gatos, but in Garden Grove. "Nevertheless," Gary says dryly, "she too wanted to be a fifty-fifty partner."

Although Gary obtained copyrights and a trademark, dozens of people knocked off their own Pet Rocks. "Unfortunately, copyrights and trademarks only allow you the luxury of spending all your time and money suing people," he comments. "For example, we got a beautiful judgment awarded to us from a Canadian outfit that was knocking us off. They sold, I'd estimate, a quarter of a million units up there. The judgment really looked good on my financial statement. But my CPA told me, 'You can't use that on your statement, because you're never going to collect on it.' And he was right. We never got a dime. I spent twenty-five grand on that case, won the judgment, and the company went belly-up and I never got paid."

In the frantic rush to produce and ship Pet Rocks before Christmas, it was impossible to operate Rock Bottom as efficiently as Gary would have liked. "I was using what I call the World War One method," he says, "just throwing more bodies into the machine guns. We didn't have time to get sophisticated. We knew the life span of the product would be very brief. You can't imagine the rush we were in to hit the retailers as hard as possible while the Pet Rock was still a hot item."

Rock Bottom was staffed during those busy months by people who were between jobs, or wanted extra money for Christmas. Gary admits that "a lot of money fell through the cracks. We could have run a tighter ship, but we were panicked. We knew we had to fill as many orders as was humanly possible while the item was still selling."

On Thanksgiving Day, Gary was in New York when he received a call from his office. The latest projection was that another million Pet Rocks could be sold. Gary's first instinct was to plan on half a million; they finally compromised on 750,000. "My figure was just about right," he says. "It was probably the best decision I made on the Pet Rock. We sold damn near all of them."

Contrary to most expectations, another three hundred thousand Pet Rocks sold between Christmas and Valentine's Day. Then it died. Gary gave most of the remaining stock to the U.S. Marines' Toys for Tots program.

"As far as I'm concerned," Gary says loyally, "it should have been a staple item on the shelf. It's the ultimate gift. But when you analyze it, I suppose it died because it got to the point where everyone had heard the joke. I remember one story I heard about an office party where everybody exchanged Christmas gifts—thirty-eight people out of forty got Pet Rocks! It was an inexpensive little gift with a great sense of humor attached. It said, 'Look how clever I am to buy this, and how clever you are for wanting it.' "

Gary Dahl, who had begun to write a paperback book for novelty stores, ended up creating a multimillion-dollar concept —a best-selling book with a one-cent rock attached. He does not claim all the credit for the success of the Pet Rock, however, but points out that in 1975 the timing was right. "The nation was just coming off Vietnam and Watergate, inflation was running high, the country needed a good laugh. One of the newspapers quoted a department-store buyer who said, 'It's the first thing I've seen in years that people will pick up and laugh out loud.' "

In spite of its popularity in America, the Pet Rock was unsuccessful in foreign countries. Its humor seemed to be uniquely American. "Furthermore," Gary comments, "we're the only people who are nuts about pets, except the English. They have a similar sense of humor, too, but they just don't have that kind of frivolous income. And in the Orient—well, they revere rocks. They pray to them. In other words, only in America!

"People ask me how I feel about all the taxes I paid on the money I made. Well, you've got to pay your dues. It's not a pleasant thing to shell out all that money, but when you stop and think about it, where but in America could I have made the money in the first place?"

The Pet Rock made such an impact on the country that its name has now become part of the vernacular. When new gift items are introduced, the standard question is, "Is it this year's Pet Rock?" Thanks to Gary Dahl, gift and novelty products are now judged by a new standard—which will be around for much longer than that short-lived phenomenal chunk of marketing genius, the Pet Rock.

The Slinky®

If you stretched out a Slinky to its full length, it would cover seventy-five feet. It has been shot into space, used by executives to relieve tension, and studied in college physics classes. It is a tool for physical therapists and an inspiration for engineers (for instance, the Slinky inspired Slinky Joe, a coil antenna designed for military use). The year the Philadelphia Phillies used Slinkies to improve their finger dexterity, they won the pennant. But perhaps the most impressive fact about the innocent, lovable little coil is that it is one of a scant handful of brand-name toys to become an enduring classic. Today the Slinky is bought for children by parents who played with it when *they* were children. The Slinky has been on American toy shelves for over thirty years—and there is every indication that it will be with us thirty years from now.

The Slinky's amazing success is due to Betty James, a tiny, energetic woman who has brought the toy through hard times with sheer determination and grit. Betty—petite, ladylike, and smartly dressed in a beige-linen suit and striped blouse—looks like neither a grandmother nor a chief executive officer . . . but she is both. Today she heads James Industries, a company she co-founded with her husband in 1945 to market a toy which, by her own account, was discovered by accident.

Richard James, Betty's husband, was employed as a marine

engineer at the Cramp Ship Yard in Philadelphia in 1943. One day while he sat at his desk trying to work out a problem, a torsion spring happened to fall off a shelf. The spring itself was one described technically as "zero compression and zero tension"—in short, no sex appeal at all. But it did not just fall, *klunk*, off the shelf. Instead, it walked across a row of books and bounced to the floor. As Dick commented later, "I didn't invent the Slinky; it practically walked into my life."

Despite its quiet ways, the coil had approximately as much impact on the young mechanical engineer as the apple did on Newton; when he saw what it did, the proverbial light bulb flashed above his head. That night he rushed in the door with the spring.

"I think we've got something here!" he announced, coaxing the spring down a few stairs. "Maybe we can make a toy out of this."

All Betty could think of to say at the time was, "What *is* it?"

The young couple and their one-year-old son, Tommy, played with the spring most of the evening, and Dick talked about its potential. Betty didn't have to think about whether to support the idea; she knew her husband was a genius.

"Whatever you want to do with it," she said, "you have my backing a hundred percent."

For the next two years Dick worked at the shipyards, earning fifty dollars a week, and in his spare time experimented with torsion springs. He had to perfect the right balance so that the spring would walk down the stairs every time—not just by accident; and the just-right formula for the steel was elusive. But finally he had a toy that he was delighted with; field-testing within the family (the Jameses now had two children) and on friends was successful. Everyone was fascinated with the homely toy. "So," Betty says, "we knew we had something—but we didn't know exactly what."

Far from being pessimistic, the Jameses' friends agreed, "You're gonna sell a million of 'em." Although Dick and Betty were not quite so optimistic, they did take the precaution of obtaining a patent on the new toy. Then they borrowed five hundred dollars and found a company to manufacture the first several hundred springs.

Betty leafed through dictionaries when she had time, looking for a name for the toy. Finally her eye lit on the word "slinky." "It described it perfectly," she says. "Stealthy, sleek, and sinuous. And the word 'slinky' has a great sound, too. As soon as I came across it, I knew that was the name." Betty and Dick registered the name "Slinky," displaying a business insight they were woefully lacking in other ways.

"We were green as apples," Betty recalls. "Once we had the Slinkies made up, we didn't have the slightest idea what to do with them."

The Slinky obviously could not be simply put out on a retailer's shelves; just sitting, it didn't look like anything. It would have to be demonstrated. Determined to get exposure, the Jameses approached Gimbel's in downtown Philadelphia in November 1945. The buyer in the toy department thought the toy looked interesting—and might or might not sell. At last he agreed to give the Jameses a small area at the end of one counter to display and demonstrate the toy.

The evening Richard went to Gimbel's with four hundred Slinkies, it was snowing and hailing. Betty was sure there would be almost nobody in the store. Worried about Richard's morale, she asked a friend to go to Gimbel's and buy a Slinky—at least Richard would make one sale. As the women walked through the store, "It was absolutely dead," Betty recalls. "There was *nothing* going on."

When the two women got near the toy department, they first heard and then saw a crowd of people, pushing and waving dollar bills overhead. "That's Dick!" Betty gasped. Dick James was selling Slinkies as fast as he could take the money.

Just as the Slinky had "discovered itself," it sold itself. Once Dick began playing with it, one customer had asked to try one, and then another. Soon the customers themselves were doing the demonstrating. "You can't help but play with it," Betty says, pulling out a Slinky and bouncing it from hand to hand. "Once you get one in your hands, it's like eating peanuts. You can't stop." The first customers had the same reaction. Needless to say, the Jameses were thrilled; Betty jumped up and down with excitement.

With the money from the Gimbel's sales, Betty and Dick went

to the manufacturer and ordered another thousand Slinkies to be made. For some time to come they would operate in this fashion, taking their profits directly to the manufacturer, who worked on a cash-and-carry basis. As the sales continued to build, Dick decided to quit his job at the shipyard and work full-time in the newly formed family business, James Industries.

Aside from the manufacture of the Slinky, the new business operated as a cottage industry, with Betty doing what passed for packaging. Initially, the Slinky was not boxed. The Jameses did, however, print instructions on yellow paper. One of Betty's jobs was to roll up the instruction sheet and tuck it into the end of the Slinky. As she looks around her present executive office, she smiles, recalling those days. "This important operation was done late at night on our dining-room table."

As the 1945 Christmas season rushed along, the Slinky's sales snowballed. When the *Philadelphia Inquirer* printed an article about Gimbel's success with the toy, other retailers became interested. The Jameses, working on a shoestring, personally went to each retailer to take the order and then made each delivery and immediately took the signed bill of lading up to the credit department to get paid. Without the capital to carry an inventory, they had to have the money to order the next Slinkies. Because the toy was a hot item, retailers cooperated with the cash-on-delivery method.

Like sales, the publicity began to build. One after another, such magazines as the *Reader's Digest, Fortune,* and *The Saturday Evening Post* printed articles about the amusing toy. As the articles appeared, retailers began getting requests for the Slinky and calling the Jameses to place orders.

Just when the young company seemed to be on its feet, the manufacturer dealt James Industries a blow. "He told us, 'We're going to make 'em up for ourselves and sell 'em,' " Betty recalls. The Jameses explained to the manufacturer that he could not legally do that; the toy was patented.

"Oh, yeah?" he replied. "Wait and see." While he went ahead with full production, the Jameses brought suit against him. Eventually they won the case. In the meantime, however, James Industries had been forced to go into manufacturing on its own.

The new machine Richard designed to form the Slinky was superior to that used in the past. He worked on the machine every day at his father's small pattern shop in Germantown, a suburb of Philadelphia. In addition, he manufactured Slinkies for the company's current accounts. Betty went to the shop each evening to pack the day's production and handle the paperwork. During the day she spent her time tending to their two children; she was pregnant with a third. (Eventually the Jameses had six children. "I feel as though I was pregnant for my entire life," Betty says.)

Throughout the Slinky's second year, sales increased rapidly, and more eastern markets, including New York City, were added to the list of accounts. Despite the publicity the toy had received, it was still obvious that it sold best when demonstrated; the average person had never seen it in action, since television was still not widespread and the Slinky had not yet been advertised on television. In most cases, the toy was shown in action at retailers by one of the Jameses.

Betty remembers one such demonstration in particular. A man had been hired to display the Slinky in action at Walgreen's Drug Store on Broadway and Forty-eighth Street in Manhattan; but he was spending more time out of the window, kibitzing with the clerks, than he was doing the work. "Guess who got put in that window?" she asks rhetorically. "I'd never done anything like that in my *life*—but for two weeks that's what I had to do. I felt like I was in a sideshow. All kinds of creepy people would hang around the window and make strange remarks. It was a horrible experience. But we'd been given the window, and it was an opportunity to put the Slinky in the limelight. We were willing to do anything for exposure."

Anytime the public saw how a Slinky worked, sales zoomed. Now that the Slinky is a familiar item to just about every American child, it's difficult to imagine how novel it was when first introduced. It seldom failed to draw crowds, often huge ones. One such crowd in Macy's in New York grew so large that the fire chief came to the store to break it up, since the people blocking the aisle created a fire hazard. Slinky received front-page coverage for that event.

During the toy's first year, it had been difficult to interest a sales representative in carrying the Slinky—and in any case, the Jameses hardly knew how to go about finding the right people. Their sole representative that year stored about five hundred dozen Slinkies in his warehouse, which also served the local oyster house he owned. When the warehouse burned down, disaster became an opportunity for the Jameses; they were forced "to find a 'real' rep to carry the Slinky."

In 1946 the Jameses went to their first toy fair in New York. Their naiveté was obvious. While most toy companies had lavish displays and curtains for the booths, the Jameses didn't have so much as a cloth for the fold-up table they brought. Their booth was so simple it was embarrassing, at first: a bare table with Slinkies on it. But people came to the booth in droves. Everybody wanted Slinkies. Suddenly the Jameses' biggest problem was producing enough Slinkies to meet the demand.

The young couple took the toy fair as a chance to learn how other people did things. "We were just babes in the wood," Betty says with a chuckle. "We were so dumb we didn't even know how to fill out an order blank. In fact, we didn't know we were supposed to *have* order blanks at the show. But we watched other people and learned from them." During and after the show, dozens of sales reps came to talk to the Jameses, asking to sell Slinky for them. Very quickly James Industries had representatives all over the United States. New business was no problem at all, with the sales reps and publicity both working to sell the toy.

Quickly, James Industries outgrew its Germantown location; the company put up its first real factory, in nearby Cliffton Heights. Business grew steadily until the factory too was outgrown; James Industries built a large, modern facility in Paoli, Pennsylvania.

As the forties became the fifties, the company grew and prospered. Betty and Dick were a good team, working side by side. His main responsibility was production, and she served as a "liaison person," doing everything from general office work to dealing with sales representatives. Since neither Betty nor Dick knew much about finances, they had hired an accountant from the very beginning. But for all her interest in the business, Betty's priorities were clear: family first, business second. She fixed breakfast for the children every day, and was home from the office by the time they got out of school, to spend the evening with them and bathe her young ones for bed. As business increased, the couple hired a housekeeper to do the housework and care for the children when Betty was not home. Still, these were hectic times for the young working mother.

Of those times, Betty says thoughtfully, "You know, in recent years I keep hearing this talk about liberation for women, and I have to say I really don't understand it. It seems as though young women don't want to stay home and take care of their children. They want to be 'liberated' so they can get out and work. Well, I guess I had that liberated life they wanted, although I didn't know it until the women's lib movement came along.

"But I never really wanted it. My greatest source of pleasure is my children, and all I ever really wanted was to be a mother."

Despite her feelings, Betty worked willingly to build the company; the Jameses appeared to have the perfect formula for success. The six children were growing up healthy and strong, and so was the company. Slinkies were being shipped all over the world. The toy had appeared on television as a "guest" of the first *Romper Room* program; Arthur Godfrey had played with a Slinky on camera for a Christmas toy show. A television crew had come to James Industries to film a segment for *David Brinkley's Journal*. The Jameses' hard work was paying off handsomely.

But not everything that success brought the Jameses was good. By the mid-fifties, just as business seemed stable, Betty began to see changes in her husband. While she was at last home with the children, he was gone more and more. "Money had gone to his head," she says. "It was wine, women, and song." Knowing he was running around—his girl friends even called at the house—Betty still loved him. Her efforts to talk to him about their problem were fruitless. "Excuses," she says with a gesture. "Denials." For all their prosperity it sometimes seemed things could hardly be worse for Betty.

Then, almost overnight, Dick changed again. Formerly a non-churchgoer, he met with members of "a holiness cult" from England, and was converted. Betty and his friends marveled at the change in him—surely a change for the better. He had stopped drinking, and his time away from home was spent not with other women, but with his religious friends. Betty was just a little uneasy; the change was so sudden and sweeping. Dick now refused to dance and had given up smoking. Still, as she comments, "Considering what he had been like, I thought something wonderful was happening, and I'd get my husband back home."

Dick was not back home, though. Instead, he was out evenings speaking at religious meetings. A dynamic man, he mesmerized crowds with the details of his former life. Betty herself sat in the audience more than once squirming at the tidbits he revealed, and hearing about incidents in his past that she did not want to know about.

"I was so embarrassed," she says, "I wanted to hide under my chair. I wanted to die."

It began to be clear that Dick was going as far in this direction as he had in the other direction—holiness had become fanaticism. "He was always preaching," Betty remembers. "If I made a comment about an attractive dress in a store window, he'd say, 'Vanity, vanity, all is vanity.'

"I'd say, 'I only admired the dress, I didn't want to buy it.'

"And he'd just repeat, 'Vanity, vanity, all is vanity.' "

The religion, it seemed, was not a solution, but a new kind of problem. Before long it became a financial threat to the company. Dick's relative wealth was well known to the other members of the cult, and he was often asked for money by one individual or another. In his fervor to spread the word, he financed one friend's trip to Russia and sent another couple to England. Much of the time the Jameses seventeen-room house held half a dozen "houseguests," friends of Dick's from the cult or new converts. He himself would sometimes bring people home and then go off on a trip—reminding Betty to feed them well.

She sighs. "When I would ask them how long they intended to stay, they'd always reply, 'We will not move until the Lord moves us.'

"The Lord," she continues with a little smile, "didn't always have to do it." Finally angry and frightened by the strangers, she sometimes asked them to leave. "Dick thought I was a dreadful person for that," she says. "He told me I was going to hell. And the children too."

Then there were other houseguests, hitchhikers Dick picked up on the roads at night. While he felt somehow protected from harm, Betty did not. When Dick brought home a guest who frightened her, she would take all six children to one end of the house, to sleep on the floor behind locked doors. She herself would stay up all night, listening and watching for intruders.

Dick's interest in the company was now almost entirely confined to giving away the accumulated capital and using Slinky to spread his cult's ideas. Finally, to Betty's despair, he insisted on inserting a religious tract into every Slinky before it was shipped out. The tract not only quoted the Bible extensively, but maligned other religions. Dick turned a deaf ear to her pleas that this would alienate parents and lose major accounts altogether, and ordered the workers to keep inserting the tracts.

The issue came to a head when Murray Gilbert, a long-standing representative and a friend, called. "Betty, he's got to stop putting those tracts in. Woolworth's is going to stop buying from us if it happens again." Betty told the packers to stop putting the tracts in.

A few days later, the tracts reappeared; Dick had gone to the factory and countermanded her orders. Murray called again, desperate—the tracts had to go. This time Betty was firm. And suddenly Dick caved in. He announced that he no longer cared about the business—it was all worldly—and he wanted no part of it. Betty could do what she wanted to with the business from now on. There would be no more arguing about the tracts.

It was late 1958, and there was not much business to argue about anymore. While Murray saved the Woolworth's account, and the other reps continued to work hard for Betty, the company was barely struggling along. Dick had given every cent of capital to the cult. James Industries was drained.

On February 22, 1959, a date Betty remembers well, Dick came home about eleven o'clock and called her and the two oldest children downstairs for an announcement: he was going into full-time Christian work in Bolivia.

Betty, numb with years of heartache, felt bewildered.

"Are you going to sell the business or run it?" Dick asked her.

Without thought or hesitation she replied, "Run it."

"All right," he said. The conversation was over.

In the months before he left, Dick had little to say to Betty. She learned the date of his departure from the janitor at the plant, and then he was gone. She was left with six children, the youngest just two years old, and an ailing business on the brink of bankruptcy. It was hardly comforting to receive periodic letters from Dick informing her that she was taking the six children right to hell with her—unless she joined him in Bolivia. Betty filed for divorce and looked at what she was left with.

In the mid-fifties, James Industries had flourished, assisted by very effective television advertising. When Dick converted, however, he insisted the advertising stop altogether, and sales nosedived. The year he left for Bolivia, total annual sales stood at $121,000. The inventory was down to forty-eight dozen Slinkies. The company which had employed 125 people full-time now had four employees. Rebuilding the business looked hopeless, but it never occurred to Betty to do anything else.

There was no longer enough money to maintain the substantial house they had lived in; furthermore, Betty needed support —family close by, and someone to help with the children while she rebuilt the business bit by bit. She decided to move the family to Hollidaysburg, Pennsylvania, her home town. Although her parents were deceased, she had three uncles and two aunts in the little mountain town near Altoona. She had always been close to the aunts and thought of them as "second mothers." She bought an old house down the lane from them, renovated it, and moved the children in.

The next year saw the toughest, loneliest times of Betty's life. She came home to Hollidaysburg each Thursday evening and stayed until Sunday, spending her time with the children and trying to fit in all the dentist appointments, dancing lessons, haircuts, and so on that six children needed. While it was an ordeal, the business was still too shaky to think of moving it just yet.

The five-and-a-half-hour trips back to Philadelphia each Sunday afternoon were the hardest. It hurt Betty to leave the children, even though she knew they were in good hands with her aunts. Trying not to think of what she left behind, she would think of what lay ahead—a business in shambles. One of her dreads was facing calls from creditors. Some sales reps were due back commissions for the past three years. Betty had to ask them to be patient, and promise that she would pay when she could. Fortunately, they believed her, and continued to represent the company; otherwise, it probably would have gone under.

"People ask me how I kept on going," she says. "I always tell them I had six good reasons to keep going, and only one reason to give up. So I was determined to turn this thing around."

In 1961 James Industries moved to a leased fifteen-thousand-square-foot building in Bellwood, a small town near Altoona. Bellwood was close enough to Hollidaysburg that Betty could be home every evening. The family was together again. The move itself had been stressful—"Much worse than moving a family with six kids," she comments—but it was over.

Shortly thereafter, the building in Paoli was sold. It was with tremendous relief that Betty asked Bob Lestochia, her financial officer, to stay late that night, " 'Cause we're going to pay everybody we owe!" While Bob wrote the checks, Betty wrote thank-you notes to go in the envelopes along with them; expressing her gratitude was not difficult. Her patient creditors had been a major factor in helping her save the business, and her gratitude was genuine.

With the factory close to home and the debts paid, Betty felt life now would be more serene. Then, in early 1962, she received a letter from Dick stating that he intended to take three of the children back to Bolivia—which three, he did not say. In February he arrived in the United States. For the next three months, he camped each night outside the house. The family was terrified. Almost immediately, Betty hired detectives to live at the house until Dick was gone.

In May Dick finally left—sans children. Betty and the children never saw him again. Word drifted back that he had remarried and was continuing to do missionary work. In 1974 he died of a heart attack.

Once Dick had returned to Bolivia, Betty was able to devote

her thoughts full-time to the children and the business. Often she became discouraged; although her aunts were warm and comforting, she had no one to turn to for business advice. Since she had been an only child, there were no helpful brothers and sisters. Often she didn't know what to do, but had no choice except to push on and make decisions.

One decision she made was to begin advertising on television again. In the past, television advertising had been very successful. After all, the Slinky was the perfect toy for an active, visual medium. The problem was that Betty did not have the money for the campaign.

In 1963 she asked Murray Gilbert and Dave Blank, an associate in advertising, to help her approach major retailers with a cooperative advertising plan. If a retailer would advertise the Slinky, James Industries would give the store an extra 5 percent of the toy's retail cost on every Slinky sold. The plan was presented first to one major retailer, who promised to make a decision shortly.

Betty now faced a second decision. The company's inventory was down to almost nothing. If the retailers agreed to the plan, it would hardly be possible to meet the anticipated demand for Slinkies—unless the company went ahead and built up its inventory now. On pure speculation, Betty ordered large supplies of both steel and plastic (Slinkies were also made in plastic now) and hired three shifts of workers; the factory began running around the clock.

As a week went by with no word from that first important retailer, Betty wondered about her decision. What if she had all that inventory—and no distribution? On the other hand, if she got the distribution, it wouldn't mean anything without inventory. She kept anticipating a yes.

By the end of the second week she was "a nervous wreck." By the third week she could no longer sleep at night. Material was coming in daily, three shifts were working around the clock.

"What will I do if they say no?" If the cooperative advertising plan didn't go, it would take forever to sell the new inventory. Betty envisioned losing not only what money she had saved, but also the house she had become so fond of.

Finally she couldn't wait any longer, and called the head man at the retail company. While she waited to be connected with him, the thought of him saying no raced through her head, followed by the thought of losing everything. "I've never experienced such suspense in my life," she says.

As soon as the man got on the line, he said, "Oh, I meant to call you yesterday. We're going to do it."

"I've never been so relieved in my whole life," Betty says with a warm smile.

The first retailer was crucial; other retailers followed his lead and decided to join the plan. Once again, the Slinky was advertised on television. In no time sales began to soar, and Betty was glad for the huge inventory she had created on speculation.

Like the Slinky itself, James Industries had been an up-and-down business. Now everything went up. Betty was faced with a new problem—lack of space. The little building at Bellwood was much too small, but she was still working with limited capital. While local people offered to finance a new site, Betty did not want to put the company into major long-term debt.

Finally, in 1965, a local pharmacist suggested that Betty look at some land near Hollidaysburg which was owned by the city. She thought it over and finally called and told him she wanted to see the land.

Betty's reaction to the field at the edge of town was positive, if unbusinesslike: "It's lovely."

"How much do you need?" he asked.

Having no idea how large an acre was, Betty said, "Well, six acres." She laughs at herself now. "It sounded like a pretty good number."

The pharmacist agreed. The city, because it wanted industry to generate employment, agreed to sell Betty the land for one dollar. The next day she signed the deed.

The building Betty had constructed on the site was fifty-four thousand square feet—almost exactly the size of the factory in Paoli that she sold after Dick left. Since then, another ten thousand feet have been added, and the company could use more space. Betty is cautious, however, about expansion.

Today, James Industries employs 134 people from the little town of six thousand. Other industries have followed to the area, but unbuilt-up countryside is still visible through Betty's office window. The office itself suggests a curious mixture of executive and proud mother. The walls are paneled in walnut and the floor is carpeted in red. Betty's desk is cluttered with letters and reading materials—and with photographs of the James children. Slinky awards are displayed on the walls side by side with photographs of important company events. On her desk sits a baby Slinky encased in Lucite, a gift made by her son Christopher, whose picture sits next to the tiny Slinky.

As it has grown, the company has welcomed the ideas of inventors. One result is the pull-toy Slinky. An example, in the friendly little crowd of Slinkies around the office, is a dog whose body is a Slinky. The originator of this idea, Helen Malsed, has received a royalty for seventeen years on each Slinky pull toy.

On the end of Betty's conference table sits a box of Playshapes, a variety of toy bricks. Those, and the Spinwheels hanging on her wall, are the result of James Industries' acquisition of a company called My Toy, formerly located in Wilma, Minnesota. "This is our first venture in acquiring another company," Betty says happily. "We're very excited about its potential." Acquiring My Toy has been quite an experience for James Industries. Once James people had studied the operation, the factory was moved to Hollidaysburg, and the equipment set up so that everything could be manufactured at James Industries.

What was virtually a one-woman business in 1960 has become a sophisticated company today. No longer does Betty make decisions alone; she is aided now by her oldest son, Tom, who is the company's sales manager, vice-president, and treasurer. Decisions are now approached by the two of them and other top executives in the company with a good deal more expertise.

Packaging is a good example. Tom holds a box of Playshapes (a product of the My Toy acquisition) and says, "We've changed this package so you wouldn't even recognize it. And since we did, sales have skyrocketed." Packaging, Tom believes, is just one determinant of a toy's success. The product has to be well named, and the company has to have a good reputation. "But number one," he stresses, "is the play value of the toy. How long will it hold their interest—and will they go back to it?"

The Slinky has "held their interest" for over thirty years. For a product which hit with a splash when it first came out, it has been remarkably enduring. "I used to worry about what kind of longevity the Slinky would have," Betty admits. "Sure, *I've* always been excited about it, but everybody gets excited about their own product. So I've worried over the years—unnecessarily, I suppose."

Indeed, Betty's attitude toward the Slinky and the company is still more than a little maternal. From a colossal problem that kept her away from her family, the company has become another child of sorts. "In a way," she says thoughtfully, "the business is like one of the children to me. It requires care—a certain amount of love and concern. And you go through all the things a parent goes through, the happiness and the sadness. You watch it grow like a child, and with growth there's a constant struggle.

"This business has been a part of me for most of my life. I could never retire. I'm sure they'll have to take me out of here in a wheelchair. You know, I never did have that empty-nest syndrome some mothers get when their children are grown—I still had the business."

Like a growing child, the Slinky has now and then sprung a surprise or two (no pun intended). When *David Brinkley's Journal* did a piece on the Slinky, it was noted that a Slinky was used in the first American satellite. Betty is still wondering how. The Slinky was chosen to travel proudly to Russia, in a display of American products. "And then there's the time," Betty says, "when Xerox came to us. They had fifty-five engineers working on a coiled spring, and they couldn't get it right. They came in here and in one afternoon our engineers made up exactly what they needed." Betty smiles like a proud mother.

It might also be noted that, surprisingly, the Slinky still costs only $1.19 to $1.69. Another surprise the toy pulls off occasionally—according to Betty's mail—is to walk *upstairs*. She quickly points out that she's not making any claims—that's just what the letter-writers say.

Given that it seldom walks upstairs, why has the Slinky been so widely accepted over the past three decades? "It's not gimmicky," Betty says promptly. "That's in its favor. It develops children's motor skills and imagination, so they like to play with it. It's visually interesting. It makes a noise. It moves—on its own; it doesn't require a battery and it doesn't wind up. Children can play with it for hours at a time." All that undoubtedly constitutes a good formula for a successful toy—if anyone can fill it.

Naturally, James Industries has spent many hours attempting to come up with another winner of the same stature as the homely little Slinky. But despite countless committee meetings and sleepless nights, nobody has managed so far to come up with another Slinky—a product which, in a manner of speaking, invented itself.

The Mood Ring

3

In late 1974 when Marvin Wernick received the sample liquid crystals he had ordered, he was like a kid with a new toy. "I'd touch it and it would turn blue," the distinguished executive says, smiling, "and then it would change to brown. All day long while I was on the phone I'd keep pressing my hand on this stuff. And I kept thinking, '*What* can I do with this?'

"One day I took it home and asked my wife, Helene, what she thought about it. I showed her how you could put your hand on it and your fingerprints turned colors.

"She looked at it and then at me. 'What is it?' she finally asked.

"I said, 'I think it's a multimillion-dollar idea.'

"She looked at it again and said, 'Marvin, I don't think you're playing with a full deck!'

" 'Okay, you'll see. You'll see,' I said."

As it turned out, Marvin Wernick was right. Liquid crystal, or Mood jewelry, was quite possibly the biggest fad ever to hit the jewelry industry. By November 1975, retailers were begging for any and all Mood jewelry manufacturers could ship. Mood rings were the talk of every party. "Are you in the mood? Your ring tells the truth." The American public had purchased many millions of dollars' worth of jewelry made of heat-sensitive liquid crystals before the bubble broke.

Marvin Wernick, a casual, self-possessed businessman, is not a person to be undone by fads. The soft-spoken Californian had been in the jewelry business for twenty-two years before he helped launch the craze for Mood jewelry. Both before that time and since, he has created other innovative jewelry fashions, many successful, and some more profitable for him—but none so volatile as the fad for Mood jewelry.

Marv seldom wears a tie to the office, preferring a fashionable sportshirt and slacks. He never wears jewelry, other than a watch, despite his enthusiasm for the creation of fashion jewelry. His office is located in a thirty-six-thousand-square-foot warehouse/office building in the wholesale garment section of downtown Los Angeles.

Marv entered the jewelry business almost by accident at the age of twenty-four. His sister, who operated her husband's business, the Oscar Charlin Jewelry Company, asked Marv to help out while her husband was in the hospital. Marv agreed; when his brother-in-law passed away, Marv stayed on for over ten years.

As he learned the jewelry business through his sister's company, which was basically a jobbing company, Marv began to form his own ideas about the industry. A thoroughgoing Californian, always tanned from golfing or sailing, Marv had ideas that eastern manufacturers didn't understand. Most jewelry at that time was made in New York City and Providence, Rhode Island. When Marv went to the market, he found the manufacturers could not conceive of the California market.

"People are very color-conscious out here," he explains, passing a hand over his graying hair. "So I'd tell them I wanted an assortment of colors and they'd talk about red, blue, white, and black. I'd say, 'No, I want avocado green. Aqua blue. Tangerine.' They'd look at me like I was crazy. I could read their minds: 'Oh, here's the nut from California.' "

Frustrated, and determined to apply his creative concepts, Marv formed his own company in 1962 and began to manufacture fashion jewelry on a small scale in "a little hole-in-the-wall," with a handful of talented craftsmen. "I was finally in the end of the business where I wanted to be," he says. "I wanted to create some unique products with my own concepts."

Inspired by the California love-of-color attitude, Marv manufactured a series of forty-two-inch ropes of wooden beads—Rainbow Ropes. The ropes came in twenty-two shades, from pastel pink to deeper pink to rose, and around the spectrum to the blue shades. Just as the concept was innovative, so was Marv's method of displaying the ropes; the sales representative would choose three ropes in appropriate shades and place them on a garment off the rack—coordinating jewelry with clothes. The result of this technique was that the shopper who bought the garment would almost always buy the jewelry as well. It was a new merchandising concept—the "color story."

When Marv entered the jewelry industry, fashion jewelry was sold by displaying it in "telescopes"—cases that opened up to show hundreds of one-of-a-kind samples. A typical jewelry salesman would carry as many as a dozen cases; the buyer had to wade through them one piece at a time. Again, Marv felt "the merchandise should tell a story. I felt we were selling a look, and it should be presented in a total package." Marvin Wernick Company designs were displayed in sets of beads, or chains, or necklace-earring sets, whatever the design concept was just then. The buyer ordered not a handful of isolated pieces, but a minimum package of perhaps three dozen pieces. With the jewelry "story" came eye-catching countertop displays, so that the jewelry was presented to the consumer attractively. Since Marv introduced the package method of marketing and the use of company-furnished displays, both ideas have been commonly accepted within the industry, and many manufacturers have followed his lead.

Marv's innovations characteristically sprang from an almost scientific curiosity about how things were done—and how they could be improved. One example was his interest in coordinating jewelry design with clothing design. When he entered the jewelry business, the industry as a whole operated independent of clothing fashions, apparently oblivious to current styles. It seemed obvious to Marv, however, that jewelry must be designed to complement clothing. "If dress necklines were to be heavily beaded with sequins, a necklace would gild the lily. Likewise, if women are going to be wearing their hair down covering their ears, you don't want to come out strong with earrings. A jewelry designer has to stand back and look at what's happening, but most of them are too busy in their own little ivory towers to pay attention."

Marv found three good sources of fashion clues: hairstylists, shoe manufacturers, and textile manufacturers. Hairstyles helped determine whether earrings would be worn and what kind of necklaces would be effective; they also suggested whether a formal look or a casual look would be more popular. Shoe manufacturers seemed to be "generally way ahead of the trends in fashion. They plan far in advance, so I get an idea of colors from them." Marv also found that color clues were available from the textile industry well before fashion colors were released by clothing designers.

Perhaps more than any other single factor, Marv's interest in other industries accounts for his company's success—and for his eventual discovery of the principle that led to the Mood ring. Other industries, he believes, are rich sources of ideas which most businessmen fail to tap. Observing that people commonly study only their own industry, he says, "I feel there's much to be gained by observing what's going on *elsewhere.*" This generalist temperament was already evident when, as a college student, Marv majored in art and minored in science. Throughout his career, he has subscribed to a number of trade magazines, believing that somehow, anything really interesting in another industry might apply to his own.

In late 1974, one of his magazines, *Science Digest,* carried an intriguing article about a new material—liquid crystals—which responded to heat by changing color. "I was fascinated with it," Marv recalls.

Liquid crystals were used, according to the article, in medicine and in the novelty business. Because the crystals changed color according to temperature, the material could be painted on any part of the body where cancer was suspected; the presence of a tumor would cause the crystals to assume a color different from the crystals in the surrounding healthy area. Additionally, the crystals were being used in digital thermometers, where indoor temperatures might be shown from seventy to eighty degrees, and the crystals would change color to indicate the room temperature.

Marv hastened to acquire samples in two forms: a liquid slurry which could be painted onto other materials, and a solid form already applied to plastic. As the article had promised, when he touched the material his fingerprints glowed, changing the pigment from black to brown to a brownish red. When the heat was increased, the color changed to reddish green, then greenish blue, and finally a bright, intense blue. So precise was the manufacture of the substance that it could be ordered in various temperature ranges; Marv knew that for jewelry he would want the crystals to respond to temperatures between ninety and a hundred degrees. (While the average internal body temperature is 98.6 degrees, the temperature of the skin is usually lower than that.)

By January 1975, Marv had come up with a way of using the crystals in jewelry. The solid material could be sandwiched between two pieces of metal, the top piece having a pierced design. This piece Marv envisioned as a pendant. It could also be die-cut in ovals, which were placed behind stones; seen through the stones, the liquid crystals looked like black onyx. But when heat was transferred into them from the hand, the color changes began.

Once he was sure the crystals could be used in jewelry, Marv contacted the liquid-crystal supplier and told the representative he had an idea that would develop a market for the fashion-jewelry industry—little dreaming the kind of market that would develop. The supplier was interested, and a salesman called on Marv that week.

Marv's assembly line was quick to turn out the first Mood jewelry and he presented the new line to his five sales representatives, each of whom had a showroom in a major market and a staff of about five people. Marv oversaw the design and shipment of brochures to the salespeople, and then talked to them by telephone or visited them personally. "The reception they gave Mood jewelry was tremendous," Marv exclaims. "But I was enthused, and I'm sure my enthusiasm was ninety percent of my presentation."

Marv knew that the enthusiasm of his sales representatives was not enough to turn the new product into a popular item. "If you're the creator of the item and you've got a good track record, then naturally your people are going to get excited because you're excited. Then, when your sales representatives are excited, they carry it with them right to the buyers.

"As a salesman, I can sell it to you as a buyer. I can get you high and mesmerized. I can give you a good song and dance so you'll buy the goods and put them on the counter. But the problem is that the retailer doesn't have anyone there who's going to do the same thing with the consumer. The item has to sell itself. *The magic moment of truth comes when you find out whether the consumer will buy it off the shelf.*"

Marvin Wernick Company display cards accompanied the first liquid-crystal jewelry—the Magic Indian Pendant. "Are You a Warm Person?" the display card asked. "Ask the Magic Indian Pendant."

If, when you wear it,
the magic pendant turns brown:
—you are a warm person—
If it turns green:
—you are a very warm person—
If it turns blue:
—you are Hot Stuff!
If the pendant doesn't change color at all:
—no amount of magic will help!!!

Marv explains that there was a scientific reason behind the famous color changes of Mood jewelry. "When a person is tense, his skin temperature goes down. When he relaxes, the blood starts flowing more and the skin surface warms up. So an uptight person will not experience as much color change, because his skin temperature doesn't fluctuate."

Marv's new idea of combining liquid crystals and jewelry mountings did not seem patentable to him. He explains that rarely is a concept in the jewelry industry completely unique. And while his own designs were entirely original, other jewelry people put almost identical products on the market within a very short period of time. How do such coincidences happen? "I have a theory," Marv says slowly. "If there are vibes in the air surrounding a new process or a new concept, other people in the industry are also very aware of it. They start to tune in at the same time—whether they're in Los Angeles, New York, or Miami.

"I'd seen it happen before, with Aurora Borealis, the cut-crystal beads with an iridescent coating. They came from Germany, and they'd been around for years, and we'd never really made good use of them, although they were beautiful beads. Then one season the ready-to-wear people started to come out with chiffon gowns, translucent, very diaphanous types of gowns. When I saw those dresses I thought, 'You can't put a piece of heavy metal or an opaque bead on that, but those cut-crystal beads out of Germany would be fantastic!'

"And the same time that we came out with them, almost to the week, two New York companies came out with them too. I'm certain it was a feeling in the air. Or let's just call it an awareness. It just became obvious."

Marvin Wernick Company introduced Mood jewelry at trade shows across the country in February 1975. It was no surprise to Marv when shortly thereafter other manufacturers began to surface. He sips his Coke thoughtfully and adds, "I'm not naïve enough to believe that I'm the only one who reads all sorts of magazines and trade publications, looks at various phenomena, and says, 'Now, how can I do something with that in my industry?' "

Marv is also the first to admit that, while his jewelry was successful, it was not until after other manufacturers got into the act that the craze began. A New York department store headlined its display ad, "Mood jewelry." Whether this inspired name was the brainstorm of some manufacturer or of an anonymous copywriter at the department store, the name was exactly what was needed to set the fad on fire. Marv says admiringly, "Whoever gave it the name, 'Mood jewelry' deserves the real credit for selling the consumer. It has to be one of the all-time super names of *any* product."

The inspired name had not been copyrighted; Marv's company immediately changed its tag lines from "Magic Pendants" to "Magic Mood Pendants." From that point on, all the company's copy began with, "Are you in the mood?"

The fad was off and running. By mid-1975, as many as thirty American manufacturers were mass-producing Mood jewelry, and others were importing it from Taiwan. Despite this fact, the Marvin Wernick Company couldn't manufacture Mood rings fast enough to meet the demand. "It was simply incredible," Marv says with a nostalgic expression.

While Mood necklaces enjoyed a certain popularity, far more rings were sold, probably because the wearer could see and enjoy a ring. Marv dropped his original concept, the Chameleon ring, in favor of the simple Mood ring—which, of course, did not reveal anyone's mood. Marv grins. "Nobody was selling Mood jewelry by advertising that the liquid crystals responded to body heat. It was a case of 'selling the sizzle—not the steak.' The idea of 'mood' is what gave the jewelry its sex appeal. And it was the sex appeal that made it such a tremendous craze."

After the product had been out for six months, it seemed like the whole world was making Mood jewelry. Marv had the jump on the competition; his company was already in full production when the fad took off, and more important, his products were already in the stores. As a result, Marvin Wernick Company got the lion's share of West Coast business, as well as substantial business around the nation. "Because everybody was promoting Mood jewelry at the same time," he comments, "we all benefited. It was all the promotions combined that caused the frenzy to have Mood rings. It was as if everyone pooled their promotional dollars together. Although it certainly wasn't planned, the net result was that everyone actually helped everyone else."

By early fall, the Mood ring was approximately 75 percent of Marv's entire volume. In November the fad peaked. Retailers all over the country were frantically calling to say, "We'll take whatever you can ship us." Whatever Marv sent, the buyer would be back on the telephone within a few days, reordering.

Marv believes every fad has two extremes. First, there is the overnight buildup to the point where every buyer will take all the merchandise anyone can send him. Then suddenly it's as if someone pulls the switch on the product—and you can't give it away. "With some fads, this happens in a matter of a week,"

Marv says with a shrug. "It can even happen over a weekend. Ropes—those long, beaded necklaces that were popular in the late fifties—were very, very hot. And when that fad died, it died over a weekend. One reason for this is that the market becomes saturated. Second, the *buyers* can become saturated. It's strange, but I've seen buyers turn down an item they're having tremendous success with. Suddenly they just say, 'I'm tired of it. I want to get something else in.' There's no rhyme or reason for it, but just the same they stop buying."

In the case of the Mood ring, the buying public was apparently saturated. "The Mood ring did a trick," Marv says. "So it was a nice conversation piece. All the advertising was slanted toward 'Are you in the mood?' and that's what everyone talked about. A guy would go up to a girl at a party and say, 'I see by your ring that you're in the mood.' Well, for a time that sort of thing is cutesy, and people get a big kick out of it. But after a while they get bored. They just get tired of talking about it. I think this is true with any novelty item.

"In the fashion industry, you also deal with the fact that the product is no longer unique. People want to be different. They don't want to wear what everybody else coming down the street is wearing. I have a rule of thumb: the hotter an item is, the more volatile it is. In other words, it will die a more violent and abrupt death than something that is not quite so hot."

Just before Christmas 1975, the Mood-ring bubble burst abruptly. The American public had purchased millions of dollars' worth of Mood jewelry. Practically overnight, everyone had heard the joke—and no one wanted to tell it another time. For Marv, the first to manufacture Mood rings, it had been around almost a year, although it was only in the last three months that his company had enjoyed tremendous sales volume. Unquestionably, he was one of the most successful manufacturers of Mood rings.

Then, almost overnight the Mood-ring fad died and retailers suddenly had more rings than they could unload. Manufacturers and wholesalers could not sell the rings at any price. Buyers still had their own inventories; even at a nickel apiece, they didn't want to add to them.

Marv comments that timing is a delicate question in any fad.

"Sometimes you have to decide you're willing to settle for X dollars and not be greedy. It's tough, because you're motivated by basic greed, and you don't want to get out too soon. After all, you're raking in all kinds of money. But all the time, you're wondering, 'My God, how long is this thing going to last?' It's very tough to quit before a fad peaks."

Stories circulate after every fad about people who made it all —or lost it all—when the bubble burst. A favorite anecdote within the jewelry industry concerns an importer who was having the popular rope necklaces made overseas during the last days of that fad. He had parlayed each shipment into a larger shipment, intending to take his money and run when his last, largest shipment came in. But while the ropes were coming from overseas on a freighter, the fad died. One Monday morning no one wanted ropes at any price.

The importer was in despair; he had mortgaged everything he owned to the hilt, and now he was going to lose it all. Then he got a telegram: "We are sorry to inform you that there has been a fire in the hold of the ship." The actual cost of the ropes was covered, and one half of the anticipated profit. The end result was a champagne party that night for everyone he knew.

The Mood ring, like most fads, attracted many such entrepreneurs. What causes a fad like this to take off is debatable; Marv disagrees with those who think it was a product of the times, a relief from the recession of 1974 and from the Vietnam conflict. "I personally don't believe politics or the economy has anything to do with it. People are always responsive to a good joke, and that's what the Mood ring was. I sincerely believe it would have been a success *in any year*. If an item is good, it's going to be good anytime!"

Because of his reputation as a knowledgeable, innovative businessman, Marv is frequently approached by people who want his advice. "Sure," he says, "some of them have very good ideas—but what they don't understand is that there are thousands of great ideas out there. To paraphrase Thomas Edison, success is one percent inspiration and ninety-nine percent perspiration. Once you've got an idea, you've got to implement it. You have to work out the bugs, and after you do that, you've got to figure out how you're going to manufacture it efficiently and profitably. Then the whole ball game is distribution. And once you've got that figured out, and you've got it distributed to the retail sources, and you all think it's the greatest thing ever to hit the market—it could still bomb."

As the story of the lucky importer shows, there is considerable risk in being in on any fad. Even when the fad is widely accepted by the public, nonexperts can suffer substantial losses, because fads are so unpredictable. Marv points out that nobody has the million-dollar ability to predict for certain what product will take off and when the public will lose interest. "The public is whimsical and fickle," he says. "For example, a few years ago Jackie Kennedy wore some puka shells to a ball, and just like that, overnight, they became a fashion. We were importing them from the Philippines, Guam, anywhere we could find them, because they were selling like wildfire. Then, within a matter of weeks the puka-shell fad just died."

Does Marv think the Mood ring could ever make a comeback? He smiles thoughtfully. "There's always a possibility. After all, it's like an old joke that's no longer funny—but tell it to a new audience ten years later, and everyone laughs. In the fashion business, when you're appealing to a teenage market, you've got a whole new generation every ten years.

"You know, I've had other items that were bigger for me than the Mood ring, that sold over a longer period of time. I also have a basement full of losers! You've got to take chances. You throw enough stuff up against the wall and hope some of it will stick.

"And it's those few wild, runaway winners, the excitement of giving birth to a concept that sells, which makes it all worthwhile," Marv concludes. "The dollars made or lost are just a way of keeping score."

4

The Hula Hoop® Toy, The Frisbee® Disc, and The Super Ball® Toy

Rich and Spud have been known to fly Frisbee discs down the corridors, or to stand around in the board room betting on who can bounce the most Super Ball toys into a wastepaper basket. They almost never wear coats or ties to work, and their office doors are always open. Is this any way to run a multimillion-dollar business? Richard (Rich) Knerr and Arthur (Spud) Melin, founders and co-chairmen of the Board of Directors of Wham-O Mfg. Co., think it is.

Rich and Spud became best friends in college; after thirty-five years in business together they are still best friends. They enjoy recounting the pessimistic words of their college professor: "A partnership is one of the best business arrangements in the world —but it very seldom works out." Obviously the exception to the rule, Rich and Spud, as equal partners, have turned a tiny cottage industry into Wham-O—the company that brought you the Hula Hoop toy, the Frisbee disc, and the Super Ball toy.

In appearance, the two best friends are very different. Rich is large at six-foot-four and 230 pounds, and impressive in his dark-rimmed glasses and white mustache. Spud is relatively boyish, five-foot-ten, and athletically built. But both men share a characteristic cheerfulness. Obviously, they thrive on what they do. While toys are a serious business at Wham-O, the atmosphere is lighthearted. "We want everybody to have a good time here,"

Rich explains. "We think that's the way this business should be."

The two friends have not been apart since just after their graduation from high school, when Rich enrolled at the University of Southern California while Spud went into the air force. When Spud's two-year hitch was up, he joined Rich at S.C.

Rich had a course in foreign trade (his major) in which every student was required to set up his own import-export company. For twelve dollars Rich bought stamps, letterhead, and had business cards printed with "R. P. Knerr Import-Export Company." Using a list of exporters the professor handed out, he wrote to companies around the world requesting samples.

"And all of a sudden stuff started coming in!" he says. He and Spud became interested in the possibilities, and immediately and informally Spud became a full partner. "The only reason we didn't change the name to Melin and Knerr," Rich says with a laugh, "was that we had already had the stationery printed." Soon the partners had samples of everything from chess sets to maracas, so they went to area retailers. "Believe it or not," Spud says, "we sold a few items. We got so excited that we started planning to go to China that summer. Then somebody told us the place to get great bargains was Guatemala."

That summer the young partners experienced their first business disappointment. After spending their 1946 summer vacations in Guatemala, they learned that "Basically, it was hard to make money that way." Supposedly reliable manufacturers shipped them inferior-quality goods; their export sales amounted to about two hundred dollars' worth of bicycle tires. The enterprise was saved from complete defeat by Spud's father and his friends in the lumber business who purchased, Spud says, "some lumber they probably shouldn't have taken, because it wasn't to spec. But it was good experience for us," he concludes serenely.

Upon their return, the young entrepreneurs developed a used-car business, buying old cars from people who advertised in the *Pasadena Star-News Independent*, and reselling them through ads in the same paper. Since Detroit automobile production had not yet resumed after the war, the used-car business was brisk. Before long, Rich and Spud were able to rent a small lot where they kept an inventory of two or three cars. Business was excellent; one month they made two thousand dollars apiece. But in 1947, when Detroit began manufacturing again, the demand for used cars dropped so swiftly that once again the young partners were out of business.

When Rich had graduated from college in 1946, Spud had decided to drop out, bored and irritated by classroom theory. "I wanted to get out and *do* something," he says. Reluctantly, the two partners took separate jobs, Rich in his father's industrial real-estate firm, and Spud in his father's lumber company.

Rich leans back in his chair, remembering those days. "It seems like another lifetime. After about six months, Spud and I were sitting in my folks' kitchen back on Le Droit Street in South Pasadena, and he said, 'You know, Rich, I'd rather earn two bucks a day in our own business than work for someone else.' So we decided to quit, because we'd *both* rather earn a buck or two a day working for ourselves."

With little discussion, the friends decided on their next venture. They would enter the sporting-goods business with a simple product that related to an unusual hobby—falconry.

Spud's interest in falconry had begun in high school and flourished when he was stationed at an air-force base in Arizona. "I used to raise and train sparrow and redtail hawks," he explains, "and I kept several of them in the barracks. I fed them cooked meats from the mess, but they'd get rickets if they didn't get fresh meat once a week or so. So I made a slingshot out of plywood, and I'd go hunting for blackbirds to feed my hawks."

When Spud came home Rich took up the hobby with enthusiasm, teaching the birds to dive for meat shot into the air. When the young entrepreneurs decided to go into business for themselves once again, they knew the red plywood slingshot was the product they wanted to manufacture.

"We bought a band saw from Sears and Roebuck," Rich recalls, "seven dollars down and seven dollars a month. Spud would cut and I'd sand, or I'd cut and he'd sand, out in my folks' garage. Then we'd both go out and sell them to local toy stores. We were making just what we'd said—a dollar or two a day."

Spud looks over at Rich and comments, "I still remember

those days when we'd both pound the pavements, going from store to store, and compare notes at the end of the day. There were days when neither of us had a single sale!" Often frustrated and discouraged, the young partners still managed to keep each other going. "When I was down," Spud adds, "Rich would pep me up, and then there were days when I'd have to lift his spirits."

Rich continues, "Then one day my barber said to me, 'You know, you guys ought to run an ad on those slingshots in *Popular Mechanics.*'"

The idea of advertising changed the concept of the product. Now it was not a toy, but a hunting slingshot, which would be purchased by falconry enthusiasts and other sportsmen. The partners paid an artistic college buddy three beers in return for drawing up the first ad. They priced the slingshot at seventy-five cents. As for the name—Spud demonstrates, holding back his right hand and releasing an imaginary sling—"Wham-O!" The sound the slingshot made became the name of the slingshot, and then of the company.

The response to the first ad was good, and the enclosed customer payments made it possible for Rich and Spud to buy more plywood and red paint and manufacture more slingshots, so that they avoided the cash-flow problems that plague most young businesses. They placed more advertisements, adding *Sports Afield* and *Field and Stream* to their market. They raised the price of the slingshot to $1.00, and then to $1.50.

The fledgling business was still very much a cottage industry. Both men's girl friends helped with the typing and other paperwork. College friends dropped by to kid around, and stayed to work on the assembly line in the garage for a salary of one quart of beer an hour. "We had a good time," Rich says. "I remember one time there were about five of us out there, and some guy who was walking by thought there was a party going on and he joined us. We just sat him down, gave him some beer, and put him to work making slingshots!"

At first the business in the garage didn't seem to have a great future; on more than one occasion, both sets of parents commented that they didn't send their sons to college to sit around making slingshots and drinking beer. But once business showed potential, it had the full support of family and friends.

On a typical working day, Spud and Rich would manufacture slingshots for a few hours and then, as Rich says, "put on our salesman's hats and call on sporting-goods stores." The next step was to hire manufacturers' representatives to do the selling. Wham-O ads began to read, "Send your money direct, or run down to your local dealer." When the dealers were shown these ads, they were more inclined to buy.

Gradually, Wham-O added related sporting-goods products: a throwing knife and a crossbow. The company had found its niche, manufacturing and distributing esoteric sporting novelties. Over the years to come, Wham-O manufactured everything from water skis to safety heaters for campers to golfing aids.

As they added new products, the partners developed their criteria. A product had to appeal to the consumer through an ad. It had to be something that could be economically shipped without damage. They never argued about whether a product would sell. When they disagreed, their motto was, "Let's advertise and see if it'll sell."

When Wham-O grew too big to operate out of the garage, Rich and Spud moved it into its first independent headquarters, an old vacant grocery store in nearby Alhambra. At first, Wham-O continued to operate mainly as a mail-order house. Spud points out that mail order is an economical way to begin a business. The partners had only six hundred dollars invested in their company when they started. Furthermore, "we were always financed by the consumer. We'd just make slingshots to fill the orders."

The slingshot remained the hottest item in the line for some time to come. To promote it, Rich and Spud took a step which would be vital to the promotion of later Wham-O products— they formed a national association. A friend, Tom Box, was head of the association, and the three young men worked to turn slingshotting into a national sport. While the association never grew large, Rich and Spud came away convinced that national promotion of that sort could be a tremendous boost for the right product when they found it.

Wham-O's progress from sporting goods into toys was slow and natural. Often toys developed from the existing line. One slingshot, for instance, came with suction-cup darts that would stick to a special target. Other toys were brought directly into the line. One such was the Pluto Platter® flying saucer.

Rich recounts the apparently ordinary day when he and Spud discovered the product. "We were down on the beach and we saw this flying disc going through the air. And it looked like fun. Well, we were always interested in anything that looked like fun, so we asked where it came from, and the guy told us he bought it at the local Los Angeles County Fair."

At the fair, Spud and Rich found a man named Fred Morrison who, with his wife, was selling the discs at local fairs. Because they liked the idea, the partners obtained rights to the disc and sold it through the trade, paying Fred Morrison a royalty on every one sold.

The Pluto Platter flying saucer was introduced by Wham-O in 1955. As Rich explains, "The sales were very low. The public didn't know what to do with it. Everyone was used to throwing a ball, but a disc? We found out that unless a salesman demonstrated it, it just didn't sell." They also found that when Fred Morrison had done a fair in the area, people knew how the discs worked, and the discs would sell in local stores. "But it was *very* slow getting started," Spud affirms.

The partners were frustrated by the lack of public reaction. "I remember going to the beach," Spud says, "and throwing the disc around, and people would just stare. And I'd wonder, 'What's wrong with these people? Don't they want one of these?' " The disc remained just another item in a line of products—an item the partners thought should be big, but that just wouldn't take off. Later, after a group of expert disc throwers (who demonstrated the product extensively at the World's Fair) had been developed, sales increased.

Soon after the frustrating introduction of the Pluto Platter, a friend brought Rich and Spud a bamboo exercise hoop from Australia. When they began to research they found that exercise hoops were not a new idea; the American Indians had used them, for example, but they were unknown to the general public. One of Wham-O's key employees, Dick Gillespie (now Vice President Operations and Products), was the first at Wham-O to learn how to use the hoop.

The partners loved the hoop, which they quickly christened Hula Hoop®, for obvious reasons. They knew they had a winner this time. But in spite of their enthusiasm, almost every buyer assured them it wouldn't sell. Still, Spud and Rich were convinced enough to take the trouble to apply for a patent and trademark on the Hula Hoop toy. It seemed like a waste of money; at the Pan-Pacific Trade Show demonstrations drew crowds of interested onlookers, but only three hoops were sold in a two-day period.

Then Spud found out what was needed to launch the Hula Hoop toy. After his kids could do the Hula Hoop, he put the Hoops in a local toy store. Then, when he and his wife took their kids to the park to demonstrate, a crowd of kids gathered, eager to try the new toy. After that, "the local stores just sold them like crazy! So we found out that whenever we gave a kid one and he learned how to use it, he was a walking advertisement. All the other kids wanted one too. At every party, beach gathering, family picnic, luau, we all took Hula Hoops and taught all our families, friends, and even passersby to do the Hoop. In other words, you gotta show 'em how it works in order to sell 'em, it's that simple. They won't sell on the shelves if people don't know what to do with them."

Quickly they devised a promotion for the Hula Hoop toy. The salesman would give free Hoops to area children who learned how to use them. The result was a chain reaction that literally spread from block to block across a city. The Hula Hoop caught on first in southern California; from there it was sent across America to take one city after another by storm. Salesmen in each city demonstrated Hoops in the local parks, and the craze spread like wildfire.

By March 1958, Wham-O's Hula Hoop toy was a national fad. Television was just coming into its own, and Wham-O was among the first toy manufacturers to advertise on the new medium. The Hula Hoop toy, a product which had to be seen in action, was perfect for television. Wham-O ads showed the naturally sexy movement of the Hoop around the waist, but toned down the suggestiveness by also showing demonstrations of Hoops around the neck and knees. The commercials showed how to roll the Hoop, run in and out of it, slide it over obstacles, and even play a giant game of horseshoes with it.

Although Wham-O had applied for a patent on the Hula Hoop toy, it had not yet been issued, and the demand for hoops was so great that Wham-O could not keep up with it. Over forty competitors entered the market; as Rich says drily, "Everybody with an extruding machine began shoving out plastic hoops."

The hoop was probably the largest-selling toy ever, and many people doubt that any future toy will match its sales. It's been estimated that during the 1958 craze alone, over 80 million hoops were sold. The whole world was caught up in the craze. Wham-O itself set up plants in Germany, Canada, and England to try and meet the demand. "But we had no management," Rich says, "and we were quite naïve in many ways. We know that now. We simply expanded too fast and too far, and very quickly the world was saturated with Wham-O Hula Hoops and hoops made by others."

Although Wham-O had originated the Hula Hoop toy and painstakingly promoted it, the company lost money on the product. "But we learned a lot," Spud emphasizes, shaking his head. "I figure that's the year I finished my college education." Typically, Rich and Spud looked for what they could salvage from the Hula Hoop toy disaster. Most important, they decided, they had learned how to generate publicity for unknown products. For instance, they had developed a technique of sending teenage boys and girls to television stations to instruct stagehands (and any other interested bystanders) on how to use the Hula Hoop. The resulting commotion often led to news coverage of the product. It was a technique that would work in later years on the sleeper in Wham-O's line, the Pluto Platter flying saucer.

Despite Wham-O's initial loss on the Hula Hoop toy, the fad had two other significant results. First, it got the company irrevocably into the toy business. Second, it made the name Wham-O familiar to the American public. In 1966, eight years after the initial Hula Hoop toy craze, Wham-O engineered a comeback of the Hoop. "With a toy," Rich explains, "you've got to remember that every seven or eight years there's a new crop of kids." The second time around, Wham-O made money on the Hula Hoop toy; since then, although the Hoop is not a major item in Wham-O's line, it is a predictable source of annual sales.

Meanwhile, the Pluto Platter flying saucer was still around. Wham-O tried new names, hoping to boost the lagging sales. Calling it The Wham-O Plutto Platter did not seem to help. A larger disc called The Sputnik was no more successful, nor were discs christened with the names of all the planets.

By 1961 Wham-O had owned rights to the disc for four years; the partners decided to find a new look for the product and promote it heavily. Rich, puffing on a cigar, tells the story with great enjoyment. "There was a famous cartoon character called Mr. Frisbee, and in the cartoon it would always say, 'Don't be a Frisbee.' Well, we thought it was such a funny name that we'd go with it." In the meantime, the product itself had been improved, with considerable attention given to aerodynamics; the partners believed that nobody could turn out a disc that worked nearly as well.

"So," says Rich, "now we had what we considered a masterpiece of a product." The partners applied techniques that they had used in promoting the slingshot and the Hula Hoop toy. Wham-O sales representatives recruited campus representatives, who earned extra money by distributing Frisbee discs and teaching other students how to use them. Rich himself did some of the recruiting; he remembers that "Yale was a natural. They had been throwing tin pie plates at the time."

The Frisbee disc, like the Hula Hoop toy, was promoted in the parks; this time Wham-O worked closely with Park and Recreation departments, not only giving Frisbee discs away, but later sponsoring competitions.

Rich and Spud do not take all the credit for the amazing success of the Frisbee disc, which has become a staple American sport. They point out that, first, the Frisbee disc is adaptable to almost any facility, indoors or out. Second, it is inexpensive, while the cost of entering many sports is relatively high. As Spud says matter-of-factly, "From a standpoint of long-time play value, everyone knows that the Frisbee disc has got to be the world's best buy." Third, the Frisbee disc naturally builds sociability, bringing together people of different ages and interests. Fourth,

Its light weight and portability mean that the Frisbee disc can—and does—go almost anywhere. "It's a great way to make a friend," Spud says, admiring a new Moonlighter® model that glows in the dark. "You can take it anywhere and get it out and find someone to play with Frisbee discs. Boy meets girl. Whatever."

The Frisbee disc's knack for breaking the ice is so well recognized that the Peace Corps used Frisbee discs as a way for representatives to befriend children in strange countries. Frisbee discs are also sold abroad; Wham-O presently has licenses in Japan, England, France, Germany, Austria, Denmark, the Netherlands, Sweden, etc. While Wham-O has also explored the possiblity of exporting Frisbee discs to Russia, trade has proven impossible, since Communist importers are forbidden to pay royalties. Rich grins. "I understand that in Russia the Frisbee disc is like Levi's® jeans. It's a crime to smuggle either one in. I've heard that before the Common Market, American kids could take Frisbee discs along when they went to Europe and get enough for them to pay for their trips." In other words the Frisbee disc, the all-American sport disc, is spreading around the globe.

In part because of the enormous success of the Frisbee disc, it is now manufactured in headquarters which are quite a contrast to the garage on Le Droit Street. In Wham-O's present facilities, manufacturing, warehousing, and distributing take place in a long 250,000-square-foot building, to which the corporate offices are attached. Wham-O has established the name "Frisbee®" as the number-one brand name for flying discs.

Rich is quick to say with a little smile that throwing discs is not all fun and games. "If we're going to brag about the Frisbee disc, I think I should tell you about Frisbee disc finger. You've heard of tennis elbow? Now there's a Frisbee disc finger, too. You get it from playing with a Frisbee disc day in and day out."

The fact that there really is such a malady as Frisbee disc finger is testimony to Wham-O's promotion of the flying disc. Over a million youngsters in more than a thousand cities participate in the Junior Firsbee disc program every year. Frisbee disc tournaments are conducted at local, city, state, and regional levels. Regional winners enter the national championship, where

Wham-O awards substantial prizes, including scholarships. The competition includes many categories: Frisbee® Golf, Guts Frisbee®, Ultimate Frisbee®, Freestyle and Distance.

The World Frisbee disc Championship, an annual event since 1974, attracts the brightest stars in the world of Frisbee disc competition. The contest, held in the Rose Bowl in Pasadena, draws as many as forty thousand spectators. The International Frisbee disc Association, formed in 1967 by a handful of enthusiasts, is now worldwide, with an estimated seventy thousand dues-paying members and even its own newsletter. The Frisbee disc, obviously, is here to stay.

Frisbee disc Golf, a relatively recent Wham-O promotion, has rapidly grown in popularity. It is Spud's favorite Frisbee disc game. Modeled on the game of golf, it has eighteen "pole holes" laid out with many hazards—trees, lakes etc.—which make necessary the mastery of a variety of Frisbee disc throws, such as left and right curves, floaters, rollers, etc. Several hundred courses designed by Ed Headrick have been built in public parks across the country. Headrick, former Vice President and General Manager of Wham-O, is the inventor of the Disc Pole Hole®, which he manufactures and sells. The game is so popular that in many colleges, students referring to golf automatically distinguish between "ball golf" and "Frisbee disc golf."

Rich's favorite Frisbee disc phenomenon is the annual K-9 Catch 'n Fetch® Contest. Currently (1981) co-sponsored by Wham-O, General Foods, and Park and Recreation departments throughout the United States, this nationwide contest attracts thousands of canine Frisbee disc experts every year, who compete in local, state, and regional competitions. Winners go to Los Angeles for the world finals; last year's winner was a whippet, Grandma Joseph. "You ought to see these dogs," Rich exclaims. "They run, they jump—they really go! They're beautiful! I'm sure many of them absolutely live, dream, and die for these contests." The Catch 'n Fetch® Contest is well established in the world of dog owners, and many dogs compete year after year and are famous for their Frisbee disc skills.

All national championships, canine or human, are attended by either Rich or Spud, or occasionally by both men. They admit to still feeling proud when they see their product being enjoyed. "I suppose we're more used to it now," Spud adds, "but in the early days I'd see people and think, 'Wow, look at that! They're playing with a Frisbee disc!' and I'd actually stop the car and go over and talk to them." I just couldn't get over the fact that people were having fun with our products!"

Another major Wham-O product is the Super Ball® toy, which was brought to Wham-O by its inventor. Rich and Spud recognized the value of the ball that bounced amazingly high, but Wham-O engineers had to overcome a problem: the ball would often break on impact. In 1965, when Wham-O released the perfected Super Ball toy, public response was gratifying, and the item still remains in the product line. The original package showed a boy bouncing the dark-colored Super Ball toy over a house. Spud laughs at the memory. "Everybody who saw that said, 'It's gone. The ball's a dark color, it's in the backyard now, they'll never find it!' " The year they were released, Super Ball toys were the biggest-selling toys in the country.

When Rich and Spud named the resilient toy Super Ball®, the word "super" was not yet in common use. At that time, the famous Super Bowl was still called the NFL/AFL Championship Football Game. Rich enjoys pointing out that he read in a newspaper that "one day Lamar Hunt, then owner of the Kansas City Chiefs, saw his daughter playing with this ball and asked her what it was. She told him, 'This is my Super Ball.' Well, Hunt thought the word 'super' was just perfect for the pro football championship, so he, then other club owners, then the press, and finally the public, began to call it the Super Bowl."

Despite the fact that Wham-O has had successful fad products, the company's emphasis today is on marketing a stable line of toys. Consequently, annual earnings have not fluctuated as much in recent years as in the past. Whether they are potential fads or staple items, Wham-O actively seeks new action toys. All employees are constantly reminded to be on the alert for new ideas.

Successful Wham-O products include the Super Stuff® toy, the Trac-Ball® toy, Zillion-Monster Bubbles toy, and the Super-elasticbubbleplastic® toy. The company makes a concentrated effort to develop brand-name recognition on all products, and to protect such brand names as Frisbee®. "The discounters want name-brand products these days," Rich explains, "not off-brands." To an extent, this has protected Wham-O in recent years from knockoffs of its products.

For every successful product Wham-O has developed, there are numerous failures. Although products are tested thoroughly before they become part of the Wham-O line, many fail to make a dent in the market. "The rate of failure is especially high when you're dealing with fads," Rich explains. "And there are so many areas in this business where you can make a mistake. But you have to be willing to make mistakes, or you'll never try anything. This business is definitely not for the meek. Ideally, it's simple; you want to minimize your risk and maximize your profit. But it doesn't always work out that way."

Although Wham-O also develops its own products, most new ideas come from amateurs, rather than from professionals within the toy industry. The inventor of the original Frisbee disc, for instance, was a former building inspector; the man who came to Wham-O with the formula for the Super Stuff toy, a compound used to block out water from oil shafts, was an oilman. "We work like a spider with its web out," Spud explains. "If we let everybody know that we're interested in seeing new ideas, once in a while we'll come across a good product."

Rich cautions, "Not too many new toys make it big. The chances of coming up with something terrific are maybe one in five thousand." Two spacious display cases in the lobby outside the executive offices hold a variety of products made by Wham-O over the years—failures as well as successes. The brimming cases contain just a sampling of the hundreds of items Wham-O has released. Rich points out, "We keep the failures here, too, to remind us that it's all part of the business, and that we're always looking for something new and different." The informal Wham-O atmosphere encourages creativity. "In fact," Spud says chuckling, "my door is likely to fly open any minute with someone running in with a crazy idea."

Although no one has a formula to determine for certain whether a product will succeed or fail, Rich and Spud have developed criteria based on experience. Most successful Wham-O toys have had a wide age appeal. Safety, of course, is of primary importance in the design of all Wham-O products.

Successful Wham-O products have also been toys which appealed to a wide audience, often to adults as well as children. Appeal to adults, however, is no guarantee of a toy's success. One example of that is a giant bird Wham-O developed some years ago. The bird had a two-foot wingspan and a rubber-band motor; it flew by flopping its wings. "Do you know who liked it most?" Spud asks. "The engineers. The guys at Lockheed were wild about it! But the kids didn't think so much of it. They'd say, 'A bird, that's nothing. I want an airplane.'" Rich adds that the product had another fault. When the bird landed, the neighborhood dogs and cats would pounce on it. Some mothers complained to Wham-O that the dog ran off with the toy bird. "It was a good product," Rich says with a shrug and a smile.

But the primary test of any new toy at Wham-O headquarters is *magic*. It is a quality impossible to define. Rich says, "If a toy has magic, when people see it they say, 'Oooh! What *is* that?' Suppose it's demonstrated on TV—the person wants to get out of his chair and buy it." Rich explains that this is where the wide appeal of many Wham-O products becomes important. "A toy with that special ingredient makes an adult say, 'Hey, what *is* that? My gosh—look at that!' It appeals to the kid in everybody. A really good item attracts an adult to buy it. He may give it to the kids when he gets home, but he likes it too. It's that magic. As somebody once said, 'The difference between men and boys is the price of their toys.'"

While it is impossible to say what this magic is, it's easy to say what it's not—"It's not trickery," Spud explains, "not like a magic trick. With a magic trick, once you know the secret, it's over. It's like the Pet Rock; once you'd heard the joke it was no longer funny. What we want is a magic aura around a toy—a certain mystique and a lot of play value."

With so many new ideas to consider at Wham-O every day, it's only natural that Rich and Spud have differences of opinion from time to time. In fact, as Rich admits with a charming smile, "never a day goes by that we don't disagree about something.

But it's a good balance. Over the past thirty-five years we've learned to argue in a constructive way." The two men are still best friends; whatever their disagreements, they never carry animosities.

Their comfortable, creative relationship is obviously one of the keys to Wham-O's ongoing success. "Another," says Spud, "is the great group of Wham-O employees, some of whom have been with Wham-O over twenty-five years." Most important is the originality of the products. Rich says, "From the beginning, we always tried for something unique. We never imitated anybody else. That's one of our key principles. We always created or found products that were unique."

Spud nods in agreement. "Unique—and magical." He continues, "You know, I've heard people say that if they were stranded on a desert island with another person, providing they have food, they'd rather have a Frisbee disc than anything else. When you stop to think about it, a Frisbee disc provides an endless source of fun."

In fact, if you had to be *alone* on a desert island, you could practice the boomerang shot with a Frisbee disc. Of course, it would also be nice to have a Hula Hoop toy and a Super Ball toy.

The Erotic Baker ®

When the Erotic Baker, Inc., opened its doors in November 1977, there is no doubt that it attracted more attention than any bakery ever had. "NYC BAKERY RATES 'X'," said one wire-service headline. Associated Press came up with "SEX AND THE SWEET TOOTH—MORE SPICE THAN SUGAR." *Money* magazine featured the new establishment in an article irresistibly titled "Hot Buns." *Playboy,* more direct, called the shop "Cookie Nooky," while *Hustler* wrote about "Hot Cakes." While the staid *Financial Times* published "The Erotic Art of a New York Cake Maker," another newspaper punned, "There's Dough in Porn." *New Times* paraphrased an old Mae West line: "Is That an Eclair in Your Pocket, or Are You Just Glad to See Me?"

Outrageous—but then the concept of an erotic bakery *is* outrageous. After all, it is the first bakery in the world to specialize in artistic (but realistic) erotic baked goods.

The object of all this attention, the first Erotic Baker shop on West Eighty-third Street in Manhattan's Upper West Side, is so inconspicuous it is possible to walk past without noticing it. True, a sign on the door reads, "A BAKERY FOR GROWNUPS." But, lest any local Hansels and Gretels peer into this gingerbread house, a drawn curtain prevents anyone under five-foot-four or so from even glimpsing the goodies inside. Although bread is being molded into breasts, and marzipan into delicate nudes, the smells that come from the door of the Erotic Baker are as wholesome as its unusual proprietors.

Karen Dwyer and Patrika Brown, owners of the Erotic Baker, are far from the conventional notion of porn-shop owners—and they would be the last to call their baked goods pornographic. "They're erotic," Karen explains earnestly. "You have to realize that erotica comes from feeling good about something. We're definitely not into pornography, because it comes from bad feelings, it's negative. Somebody gets exploited in pornography. We don't exploit anybody. Erotica is about a feeling of life and joy."

Karen, an attractive woman in her early thirties, is petite and vivacious. Her brown hair and eyes are set off by vibrant colors —today a navy pantsuit and red-silk shirt with pearls. Although she has the savvy of any M.B.A., her University of Hartford B.A. is actually in music, and her career before the Erotic Baker was acting and singing in summer stock, dinner theaters, cruise ships, and clubs. Far from becoming an opera singer, her college ambition, Karen played in such hit shows as *Carousel, Oklahoma!,* and *Man of La Mancha.* It was not, as she comments with a winsome smile, the experience she needed to start a business in New York City.

Patrika, Karen's roommate and partner, also had almost no experience outside theater. A lighting designer, Patrika has done numerous Broadway shows as well as the acclaimed off-Broadway hit *Vanities.* Ten years Karen's senior, Patrika is five-foot-two, slightly plump, and striking, with shocking white-blond hair, hazel eyes, and an open, sunny face. A native of San Francisco, she dresses with casual big-city elegance in a tan-cashmere pantsuit and boots, and talks with quiet assurance, gesturing continually and stubbing out one cigarette only to light another.

The Erotic Baker was conceived in the same way other bright ideas have been—as a joke. One Sunday in May 1977, Karen and Patrika entertained some friends at brunch, and got to talking about their erotic art collection, which is quite visible in their fashionable West Side walk-up apartment. As Karen comments, "At that time our interest in erotic art was considerably stronger than any interest we had in baking—although I can't say the same today."

62

At the party, Karen pointed at one of their paintings and joked, "Wouldn't it be funny if you could eat these things?" Everyone laughed and forgot the statement—except Patrika and Karen. "It was as though two light bulbs lit up over our heads," Karen recalls. "We looked at each other and just smiled."

As soon as their friends left, the roommates began talking about the idea and how they could make a business out of it. With growing interest they discussed its potential for making money. To this day, neither one takes credit, but both admit that Karen thought of it first, and it was Karen whose enthusiasm grew rapidly. Patrika brought up very real objections: could the two women commit the necessary time to starting a business? Would they get bored after a few long weeks? And the big question: "Are we really going to follow through on this?" Before they had taken any tangible steps toward the business, both women knew it would require a demanding work schedule for any number of years—how demanding, they did not yet know.

Karen's dissatisfaction with her show-business career had been building for some time. "The theater was my whole life," she explains. "But one day when I was down in Virginia playing in *Kiss Me, Kate,* I realized I was wasting my life. I wasn't growing in the business, I'd get up in the morning and sit around the pool, and I was too lazy to even read a book. I thought, 'Wait a minute, there's got to be a brain in here somewhere. Something is wrong.'"

At that time Karen had just turned thirty, and was separated from her husband of eight years; she was restless. "So when Patrika and I began talking about starting our own business with erotic baked goods, I was really ready to do something entirely different with my life." She flashes a bright smile. "Little did I know what I was letting myself in for!"

Patrika had several theatrical lighting jobs around the country; she left town and Karen began the slow, hard work of researching the business idea. One place she went for information was the Small Business Administration, where she learned about licensing and was given books on how to set up a bookkeeping system. Figures about the potential success of an erotic bakery, of course, were not available. In fact, Karen shied away from telling anyone at the SBA exactly what she had in mind. "If I had spelled it out for them, they would have thought we were crazy!" The figures she was given referred to "regular bakeries"—how many bakeries a neighborhood with a given population sustained, for instance. Karen sighs. "Even if we had known how many people would buy a Danish, I'm not sure that kind of information would have been helpful. We just didn't fall into any of their categories. Our idea had never been done before."

In the initial stages, the partners talked to no one about their business idea. One of their fears was that someone might steal what they were convinced was a great idea. Their own capital was limited; somebody else with money could have opened well ahead of them. But they had another reason for secrecy: they didn't want any negative feedback. Patrika explains, "Even though people don't mean to, they can be negative about your plans. Just a comment such as 'Isn't that silly!' would have been very discouraging to us."

Not talking about possibilities was also an old habit from the theater world. To announce the Erotic Baker before it opened, they felt, would have been like announcing you had the part after an audition—when the contract had not yet been signed. As Karen puts it, "Only when it's in the bag do you announce it to the world."

Once they knew they would start the bakery, Patrika and Karen set a November opening as a target date. Meanwhile, Karen took courses in sanitary food handling sponsored by the city of New York, as well as a course in public relations. Patrika developed an unexpected ability with cake decorating and sculpturing; she also set up an accounting system, since she had learned accounting working in offices during slow theater seasons. Knowing the limits of Patrika's experience, the partners also decided to hire a reputable accounting firm when the business actually began.

While the pair made numerous errors in judgment at this stage, they agree that the worst was in estimating expenses. Having no experience in business, Karen made a three-month projection of the cost of rent, insurance, utilities, and so on, based on their apartment expenses. "Now, first," she says, "we should have

64

made a year's projection. And second, the costs of business are not the same as the cost of New York apartment living. *Now* we know that a commercial enterprise will pay about three times as much for electricity, rent, insurance, telephone service—just about everything!" Using the faulty projection, the partners estimated that they needed twenty thousand dollars to start the business. "And that's what we put in," Patrika affirms. "Let me tell you—we did it on twenty thousand dollars, but we could have used sixty thousand!"

Needless to say, when Karen and Patrika went out to seek financing, they caused a certain amount of blushing and snickering in New York's pin-striped financial community. However, the bankers agreed that erotic bread and cakes had a future; among others, Manufacturers Hanover Trust agreed to offer a loan. Seeking the lowest interest rate, Karen also explored the Actors' Federal Credit Union. Since Patrika had recently inherited her grandmother's house in Carmel, sold it, and invested the money with Paine Webber in assignable AAA securities, lenders were taking no risk. In the end, Paine Webber offered the best terms, and the partners borrowed the twenty thousand dollars there.

Faced with dozens of business problems for which they had no background, the two women enjoyed tackling another problem—choosing a name. They talked over this decision as they did others, evenings after work, often sitting on the couch in their Upper West Side apartment. "Not all of it sitting here," Karen adds with a grin. "A lot of this business was planned on a cocktail napkin, too." The list of appealing names was endless, with Cookie Nookie an obvious choice and Cookie Closet more innocent. One serious possibility, the Exotic Baker, seemed to the partners to conceal what the business really was. Finally they agreed to give the bakery a name that straightforwardly told what it was about: The Erotic Baker.

Naming the future products, they decided to be more euphemistic. Penis Bread was voted down in favor of His Bread. Gingerbread People and Marzipan Delights, even though nude and erotic, would be easy for people to ask for. On the other hand, what could little chocolates shaped like breasts be named but

Tiny Titties? "It's amazing how we've gotten used to this place," Karen says. "People come in here and ask, 'Are your boobs fresh today?' and I don't even realize anymore that it's funny. But *it is funny*." Whatever the products are named, some customers become inarticulate once inside the Erotic Baker. Karen dimples. "They just point and say, 'Give me that long one over there, and two of the round ones here.'"

The name "The Erotic Baker" has not been quite as problem-free as Karen and Patrika anticipated. For months the telephone company billed The Neurotic Baker. Every so often mail comes addressed to The Erratic Baker. "All of which is correct," Patrika says dryly.

One of the most important early decisions was the location for the store. The Eighty-third Street site had several things going for it. First, it was in the neighborhood, only a short walk from Karen and Patrika's apartment. Second, it was just a few doors from Columbus Avenue, a popular West Side shopping area with many fine restaurants and boutiques. Third, the rent was only four hundred dollars a month for four hundred square feet—a bargain in New York City. (Later the store expanded into a former Chinese laundry next door, gaining another three hundred square feet.)

With all this in mind, the final decision was impulsive.

"I'm not exactly sure what was here before we moved in," Karen says, shaking her head. "Supposedly it was a thrift shop, but . . . anyway, the place had been vacant for some time and it was filthy, just horrible. But when we came in to see it, the sun was streaming through the windows. And we were so darn naïve that I just said, 'Oh, it's so cute. Let's take it.' How's that for good business sense?"

The partners are fond of saying that they literally built their business—with hammers, nails, paint, and the help of friends. The dirty, neglected interior had to be spotless before the bakery could open. Patrika affirms, "When you see it today, you can't possibly imagine that it's the same place."

That fall, while the cleaning and remodeling went on, Patrika commuted from Bennington College, where she was guest-teaching two classes. She drove to Vermont Thursday mornings, taught Thursday and Friday, and drove back to Manhattan Friday night, five hours each way. Although the driving and teaching drained her energies, the money was necessary with everything going into the business and nothing coming out.

As the opening date grew nearer, the partners began to have second thoughts. At one point Patrika said to Karen, "Okay, if we turn back now, we're only going to lose the original twenty thousand dollars. We may even be able to get some of it back. But if we're going to turn back at all, we have to do it now." After they talked, the women decided to keep going.

In preparation for the opening, they hired a press agent. Having taken her course in public relations, Karen knew the Erotic Baker's start-up capital did not allow for the expense of advertising. Any publicity would have to come from the interesting nature of the shop itself.

Four days before the grand opening, everything seemed to be more or less in hand. Patrika was in Bennington, and Karen was in the store icing cakes. The plan was for the Erotic Baker to be open a few days before the actual opening, which would be publicized by a press party the press agent had arranged to be held in the shop. Karen had only one thing to worry about: an interview with a reporter from the *New York Post*.

When the reporter arrived, her first words were, "When's the demonstration?"

"What demonstration?" Karen looked outside; people were gathering across the street.

Uneasily she watched more people arrive, and then trucks from NBC, ABC, CBS, and local news media. When *The London Sun* telephoned, Karen learned that the demonstration was about the Erotic Baker.

She called the press agent and said, "Get over here right away. All hell's breaking loose!"

Far from being arranged by the press agent, the gathering was the result of complaints from one disgruntled West Side citizen who was afraid the store would be a sex shop open to children.

Karen and the press agent reassured the reporters and opened the shop. The Erotic Baker was mobbed with people, cameras, and lights. "And just then," Karen says with a little laugh, "poor

Patrika came dragging in from one of her trips to Vermont. She took one look and I could tell she just wanted to turn around and go right back out the door!"

The advance publicity was probably greater than that the arranged press party would have generated. When the Erotic Baker officially opened a few days later, everything in the shop was sold out by four o'clock in the afternoon. The partners had not known how much stock to have on hand; moreover, they could never have anticipated the crowd that stormed the door. The opening had been a success. If Patrika and Karen had purchased the publicity the demonstration created, it would have cost an estimated half-million dollars.

While the public reception surprised the two novice business-women, the work involved in the store surprised them far more. Friends had tried to warn them: "Do you have any *idea* how hard it's going to be?"

"I felt they were being discouraging," Karen says with a sigh, "and I kept saying, 'Yes, yes, yes, but I know we can do it.' Now I know they were absolutely right. I *never* could have guessed how hard we'd have to work."

Patrika gestures emphatically. "I thought, well, it will mean a ten-hour day, maybe a twelve-hour day. But not eighteen- and twenty-hour days! I didn't think it would mean not being able to find time to shower. Not being able to go home and go to bed, but having to sleep here on the floor. We had no idea this was going to happen. There were times when our feet were so swollen we couldn't stand on them anymore. And there were times we were both so tired we couldn't see. We couldn't feel. We couldn't think!"

Despite their exhaustion, Patrika and Karen never considered quitting; they were determined to succeed. Still, business seemed to be one unexpected problem after another. Because they had started their business on a shoestring, even small problems assumed the dimensions of catastrophes. As Karen puts it, "So many things we never anticipated kept coming up. An appliance would break down and cost fifty dollars to repair. To us, that was a disaster. Or a cake decorator would finish a custom-made cake and then turn around and sit on the damn thing! Or the truck driver would walk out carrying a fifty-five-dollar cake and slip, and the cake would land on his head!"

Some early disasters turned out, like the demonstration that drew so much publicity, to be blessings in disguise. Karen remembers one day when she was so exhausted that she couldn't mix another bowl of icing—her hand and arm were too sore to stir it together. "I was so frustrated I just thought, 'Oh, hell, I'll use what I've got.' So I gave the gingerbread men and women pink pubic hair instead of chocolate. Well, don't you know that people were fighting over those few cookies with pink hair!"

The partners are now resigned to the fact that being in the bakery business means periodic disaster. Patrika can't count the times she has had to drive the delivery truck because the driver walked out. Both partners remember one frantic last-minute emergency that centered around a beautiful custom-made wedding cake. The cake, completed the evening before, showed the New York skyline at sunset behind a red apple and hand-sculpted bride and groom.

"Gorgeous," Karen says. "But I looked at the cake and I wasn't satisfied with it. So the next morning at eight o'clock I came in to redo it. Well, it was very hot and the air conditioner had broken down. And everything I did with the icing just melted and fell apart. Finally at eleven I called Patrika and said, 'The wedding is in an hour and a half!' We had to completely redo the cake in that time. It ended up beautiful, but *we* ended up crazy.

"There must have been a million times when I felt so frustrated I was ready to throw in the towel. It was never lack of customers —it was things going wrong." Patrika nods agreement. "And it seemed like every time we had a major catastrophe, Patrika was out of town. Like the time the freezer—we had bought it used for eight hundred dollars—broke down, and I discovered it at three in the morning. It was full of water, food was being ruined, and I had to do something about it. Sure, I sat down to cry for five minutes. But I still had to do something about it, so I rolled up my sleeves and went to work."

Minor catastrophes often meant money going down the drain. Nothing felt worse than being unable to meet the demand for erotic baked goods because something went wrong. One such problem occurred with the bread. The women had commissioned molds to create bread shaped like breasts. The bread was very popular—but the molds were so heavy that bakers couldn't lift the trays. The initial molds had to be scrapped and another set made.

The popularity of the bread was actually a problem in the early days. Karen remembers, "People would want it so much that they would be waiting in the store for the baker to finish cooling the bread. It's a great smell, that fresh bread. The store would fill up, people would be on the street, and I'd be hysterical! We'd serve them coffee, anything to keep them happy! But they were impatient; they wanted bread. In the meantime, here we were, thinking we were hostesses at a cocktail party instead of running a business."

Karen and Patrika painstakingly designed all the molds for their unique products. In trying to find out how molds were made they encountered problems, "simply because we were women," Karen says, sighing. "Men just refused to take us seriously. It was as if we were two ladies at a flea market."

Patrika agrees. "I remember saying to Karen, 'I cannot *wait* until I can pick up the phone and talk to a supplier and have him take me seriously. Why do I have to plead and beg with them to get anything done? Why do I have to ask them *please* to send our boxes? Why can't I just tell them to send the damn boxes!' "

Buying equipment was equally frustrating. When the two women went down to the Bowery where secondhand equipment was sold, they soon learned they could not give out their business cards without risking a sly remark about massage parlors. Patrika believes that men in the same position would have been treated with more respect. "They just wouldn't take us seriously because we were two women in business—and a very unusual business at that."

The partners feel that they handled these situations poorly in the beginning because, as women, they didn't understand "the game." "Somebody'd throw a ball at us and we didn't know how to throw it back. We took things at face value. We had never learned strategy," Patrika concludes.

"In fact," Karen adds, "we didn't even realize it was a game. Well, I'm not saying we know how to play the game now, but at least we recognize it more quickly."

In spite of Patrika and Karen's inexperience in the competitive world of business, the business succeeded—in part because of the strong relationship between the two partners. Before they became partners, they were close friends, and still are; they have never had a fight. They are quick to say that they disagree frequently, and sometimes strongly, but each is willing to understand the other's point of view. A simple, informal method of handling disagreements has helped them compromise. Patrika explains, "No matter how badly one of us wanted to do something, if we couldn't compromise we didn't do it. But it's almost never come to that. It's amazing how rarely there's an issue that we don't get together on."

Like most successful partners, Karen and Patrika have different strengths and areas of expertise. Patrika, more adept at bookkeeping, is also the one with real talent for sculpturing cakes; all along she has been responsible for training other sculptors. Karen adds that Patrika is "the efficiency expert. It's amazing how she can come up with formulas that make things work around here."

Karen, with her background in acting coupled with her charming personality, excels at public relations. She also has a knack for purchasing the sideline products that have turned the Erotic Baker into a bakery-boutique. Since people frequently buy fancy baked goods for birthdays and other occasions, the store carries a line of greeting cards. Other erotic goods include pot holders, mugs, an X-rated cookbook, and risqué fortune cookies.

The casual partnership has been so successful that in April 1979 a second Erotic Baker opened in Greenwich Village. In September 1980 a third shop opened on Fifty-first Street between Second and Third avenues—what Karen refers to as "our East Side chic shop." As part of her responsibilities, Karen makes the rounds of the two new shops, spending at least three days a week visiting them. All three shops are overseen by general manager Peter Turchiano, an old show-business friend who joined the Erotic Baker during its second year.

No one is more surprised than Patrika and Karen at the fact

that the Erotic Baker now has three locations. As Patrika puts it, "When we started out, we planned to have just one store that would be run by the two of us—a small business with a low overhead. I would continue to do my shows out of town, and Karen would tend the bakery. We hoped to make a good living at it. But no way was it supposed to be three stores in three years."

Three stores is the maximum New York City will support, Karen and Patrika believe. As it is, the three stores now draw people from far beyond Manhattan Island; many steady customers come into the city from Long Island, New Jersey, and Connecticut, and make the bakery one of their stops. New York is also a good location because of its tourists, many of whom don't want to go home without something from the Erotic Baker.

Although the partners know their artful, edible erotica have been publicized nationally, they are still sometimes surprised by long-distance business. One customer called Karen, for instance, to order a custom-made surprise birthday cake for her husband. Karen took the order and then asked when the cake had to be ready.

The woman said, in an accent right out of *Gone With the Wind,* "Well, Ah have to have it down heah in Nawth Calina—"

Karen interrupted, "I'm sorry, but we don't deliver."

"Oh, that's all right, honey, mah husband's flyin' up there in his Lear, and he'll just bring it back on his lap."

"And he did," Karen confirms with a delighted smile. "He came in and got the cake, promised not to look in the box, and took it back home in his private jet."

The Erotic Baker attracts many people visiting the city, including celebrities. Among the customers who have sampled its wares are Jane Fonda, Bianca Jagger, David Bowie, and Lucie Arnaz. The store has made cakes for numerous celebrities; the first, a copy of the poster from *The Act,* was ordered by the designer Halston for Liza Minnelli's birthday. The shop does a significant business in nonerotic cakes, too. One charming cake, ordered by Diana Ross, depicted her daughter's bicycle. Another was ordered for Brooke Shields' sweet-sixteen birthday by Calvin Klein.

One of the most amusing and complex cakes the Erotic Baker has ever made was ordered for a New York Knicks gathering. The woman who picked the orgy cake from the shop's catalog asked that it be customized to represent individual players in various and sundry positions on a basketball court, and in different states of undress. Some had only T-shirts on, some had only socks—but all were easily identified by their numbers! The huge cake ultimately fed two hundred guests—after it had entertained them.

One of the most expensive cakes ever made was created by the Erotic Baker for Stephanie Mills, the young actress who starred in the Broadway production of *The Wiz*. Ms. Mills' fellow cast members ordered a sixteen-foot-long yellow-brick-road cake delivered to the New York, New York disco. The cake arrived in sections, accompanied by many bowls and tubes of icing and bakers in their smocks. The cake, set up on a specially built ramp with flashing lights around it, was presented to Ms. Mills and pronounced a great success. The price tag: one thousand dollars. "It was a work of art!" Patrika says, glowing with enthusiasm. "But then, all of our cakes are."

It was probably inevitable that the Erotic Baker would be asked to create a cake for *Oh! Calcutta!*, the long-running erotic musical. The cake depicted the Broadway play's logo, a naked Maja in a prone position. Cookies from the Erotic Baker were also sold in the lobby of the theater; some had the name of the play written across them, and others were gingerbread people wearing hot pants made of pink icing. Though the cookies, which were often saved as mementos, generated good publicity, selling them in a theater lobby presented such a breakage problem that the operation had to be discontinued.

Since *Oh! Calcutta!*, the Erotic Baker's first experience in selling its merchandise outside its stores, other distribution channels have proved more successful. The company now has a growing mail-order business and a thriving wholesale business. Karen is president of the wholesale company, while Patrika is president of the retail company. Although the retail end of the business receives most of the publicity, Patrika and Karen anticipate that the wholesale division will eventually generate the most revenues.

In developing the wholesale company, Karen has attended numerous trade shows. Erotic candies and color postcards of erotic baked goods are now sold by manufacturers' representatives to gift shops, card shops, pharmacies, small boutiques, and lingerie shops. Cakes are not wholesaled, since their shelf life is poor, especially in warm weather, and shipping would be a problem.

As the Erotic Baker's products have become nationally known, Karen and Patrika have had hundreds of inquiries for franchises. They feel, however, that quality control would be impossible in their business, and have not been willing to franchise. They are considering expanding to other major cities, such as Chicago, San Francisco, and Los Angeles, but if they do, the stores will be company-owned.

The Erotic Baker's one attempt to "go international" was comic but not very successful. A gift-shop owner visiting the New York Gift Show ordered some merchandise shipped back home to London. Some weeks later Patrika and Karen received a letter from the customer: "You're not going to believe this, but British customs impounded everything for being obscene." Karen still shakes her head at the story. "I'm sure the customs officers had a wonderful time with everything." Another customer reported giving a gingerbread cookie to an Italian customs officer who thought the cookies were hilarious. At last report, the erotic cookie was still hanging on the wall in Italian customs.

Some people buy the Erotic Baker's goods with no intention of eating them. If dried, the breads and marzipan sculptures can be coated with polyurethane and framed—and they often are. Patrika laughs. "Our motto is 'Eat it or keep it.' Of course, it's not unusual for someone seeing a loaf of bread shaped like male genitals or a breast for the first time to ask, 'How could anyone actually cut into that?' "

There's no question that the Erotic Baker's goodies are not just tasty, but titillating—and certainly more explicit than what Grandma used to bake. The gingerbread cookies are not for children—both male and female come with sexual organs intact. In addition to bread shaped like breasts or genitals, there is marzipan candy in a variety of shapes and colors, from red lips to artistically molded rear ends. Lovingly detailed renditions of the clitoris can be had in chocolate as well as other flavors. For those who are into SM fantasy, there are feathered whips made out of licorice. And what goes on a custom-made cake is limited only by the customer's imagination.

One popular cake is shaped like a breast, with a frosted message reading "Breast Wishes on Your Birthday." More suggestive cakes show couples making love; one motto: "Let's Bang in the New Year." In the candies, the Chocolate Big Boy in white chocolate with a cream filling is popular, and the red marzipan mouth, complete with a sensual pink tongue, is a top seller. Surprisingly, the majority of customers are women; the most popular items are the gingerbread cookies and cakes shaped like breasts. Many women also buy breast cakes for their boyfriends or husbands. Cakes in the shape of buttocks are popular, too, especially when inscribed "Bottoms Up."

Karen and Patrika put a great deal of effort into designing something new and different each season, both for the stores and for the sales reps to show. One Easter, for instance, featured "Humping Bunnies" on top of a beautiful cake. Another Easter specialty was a gold papier-mâché egg with a surprise inside; the nature of the surprise was indicated by the title on the box—a Tits 'n Ass Egg. Before Valentine's Day the stores are busiest, although Christmas generates more sales because the Christmas shopping season lasts longer. One of the all-time favorite items, however, is not sold for Christmas or Valentine's Day, but for the Fourth of July. The special cake, shaped like a vagina and frosted in red, white, and blue, is called "Birth of a Nation."

The "Birth of a Nation" cake is an example of the kind of erotic art Patrika and Karen enjoy creating—beautiful, delicious, and good-humored. Karen explains, "I think it's just marvelous when I see men and women in here giggling and having a good time." Occasionally someone walks into the discreetly curtained shop seeking an ordinary Danish, and entirely unprepared for the lavish display of risqué goodies. "When that happens," Karen says, "we just tell them where to get a Danish, and they walk out."

The curtain that conceals the original shop from passersby is part of the Victorian decor; the store was designed so that customers could sit at small tables and enjoy coffee with their pastries. While the sign at the door reads "A BAKERY FOR GROWNUPS," a surprising number of people do bring their children in.

By and large, children respond to the Erotic Baker with at least as much poise as grown-ups. Younger children often don't recognize the frankly adult items displayed in the Spare Parts counter. Karen enjoys telling about "a wonderful little girl about five years old who was in here one day with her mother. She had her nose pressed against the glass, and she looked and looked. Then she started tugging her mother's arm and pointing. 'Look, Mommy, a T! Look, an O!' To her, that's what the penis and vagina breads looked like. I think that's perfectly wonderful!"

The Erotic Baker has been described as "a gingerbread house with a chic art-gallery atmosphere," and that's exactly how Karen and Patrika want it. "People come into our stores and they're having a good time with it," says Karen, beaming. "And if they're having fun, they're probably going to buy something."

Karen, admittedly, is having the time of her life as an erotic baker. "Do you know what I like about it?" she asks with a twinkle in her eye. "The fact that it's outrageous. I enjoy being outrageous. I get a special thrill when I see people buying these silly marzipan penises we thought up. And it just cracks me up to see trays of them all lined up. Even now, I still get a kick out of it." Although Patrika and Karen don't get curtain calls nowadays, they enjoy a different kind of applause. "We receive applause," Patrika says, "when we see people accept our products—and enjoy them."

Both women feel there is a connection between the sensual pleasures of food and sex. "That's why the eating scene in *Tom Jones* is so fantastic," Karen says. "It shows that connection." Not surprisingly, Karen herself once played the part of Molly in that show.

It's easy to be so fascinated by the erotic art of the Erotic Baker that you forget that these products are also good food. In fact, many customers order custom-made cakes which are not erotic —but are both beautiful and delicious. "Our cakes just melt in your mouth," Patrika says. "And however they're decorated, if they're delicious, they're erotic. One of our basic premises is that erotic does not necessarily have to be sexual. If looking at it or feeling it or tasting it makes you feel good—then it's erotic."

The fact that the products *are* delicious is one of the hazards of the business for Karen and Patrika, who both put on weight when the bakery first opened. Karen describes those days with a laugh. "I would decorate cakes and it would be, 'One for the cake, one for me; one for the cake, one for me.' We were both doing that, so we both got a little on the chubby side. We're using more restraint nowadays. But at first we were like kids in a fantasy."

It's obvious that customers, whether they're tourists from out of town or regulars, feel the same way. The Erotic Baker is a spicy fantasy come true. For Karen and Patrika, it is an absorbing dream come true. Obviously, they are having a wonderful time. "Why not?" Karen asks with a discreet wink. "After all, there are two things in this world I truly love . . ."

Food and sex—what a delicious combination!

Eastern Onion™

Walking through the long corridor that led from TWA Flight
Number 663 to the Las Vegas airport terminal, I wondered,
"How in the world will the Eastern Onion representative and I
recognize each other in the crowd?" I hoped it wouldn't take too
long. It was ten-fifteen A.M. Las Vegas time; I had been up since
four-thirty, and was already feeling the first symptoms of jet lag
—fatigue and a little disorientation. My suit was wrinkled and my
briefcase seemed to get heavier and heavier.

Ahead of me I could hear laughter and cheers from the winners playing the wall-to-wall slot machines inside the terminal. It
had always amused me that even a payoff of a few coins clatters
like a large jackpot. As I entered the terminal, several of my fellow
passengers were greeted with shouts and hugs by friends or relatives. As always, I envied the warm receptions. On most of my
frequent business trips, I walk into the terminal not knowing a
single person.

I did have someone to greet me this morning, someone from
Eastern Onion. A company employee had my photograph from
a book jacket. I could only wait to be recognized. Meanwhile, I
scanned the faces around the baggage checkout.

Then I was distracted by something I had never seen in any
airport before—a beautiful belly dancer in full costume, a figure
right out of the *Arabian Nights*. Her rhythmic gyrations were

attracting a delighted crowd. Passersby were bumping into one another as their heads turned to watch her. Some whistled or applauded as they went by. She was absolutely terrific, and she had to be to cause this kind of sensation in Las Vegas, the world capital of beautiful showgirls.

My tiredness forgotten, I watched her, wondering what lucky guy she was meeting. When she looked at me, I looked away, a little embarrassed; it was impossible to watch her without being aware of her frank sex appeal.

"Bob Shook?" she called out musically. "Are you Bob Shook?"

"Er, yes."

"Welcome to Las Vegas, Bob!" She danced over in front of me and swayed to a stop. "My name is Sue Lee. Mary sent me to pick you up."

With some relief I saw my luggage come out and we got it. As we walked through the terminal, people continued to stare; even though Sue was no longer dancing, she was still spectacular in her costume. And while I knew it was her outfit that drew everyone's attention, I felt like I was on center stage too. I knew my face was turning red. I heard someone asking, "Who's the VIP?" And some people actually did double takes. Whether they thought I was a high-rolling gambler, a show-business personality, or whatever, I had to admit it was secretly thrilling to get so much attention.

Hundreds of thousands of people have been entertained, as I was, by unexpected Eastern Onion "grams"—jazzy, sexy, funny one-man-band performances. Since the company opened its doors in Las Vegas on April 1, 1976, it has become the largest singing-telegram company in America, with thirty franchises across the United States (including Hawaii) and Canada.

By her own admittance, trim, attractive Mary Flatt, Eastern Onion's founder, is an unlikely candidate to run any business. She started the company with no business experience to speak of, virtually no capital, and a history of failure in almost every line of work she ever tried. She smiles wryly as she talks about it now. "When people complain that they don't have what it takes to own their own business, I tell them, 'I'm a woman in my early thirties. I have no college education. I have two sons and a husband. I'm brown-skinned [being Irish and Filipino]. So what excuse do *you* have?' "

Mary did have one unbeatable asset, however—an enthusiasm that is evident in her rapid-fire speech and dramatic gestures. Nevertheless, in a pretty Indian silk dress and with her brown hair worn Afro style, she still looks more like a sexy Eastern Onion messenger than the chief executive officer of a national company.

Nothing in Mary's background prepared anyone for the amazing success of Eastern Onion. A vivacious woman, Mary has just about enough energy to outwork three ordinary people. But that didn't bring her success for many years. "My business background," she says with a shrug, "is a joke. I never lasted longer than six months at any job. I did everything—accounting, waitressing, bartending, working as an employment counselor. For five years I stayed home housekeeping. But whatever I did, I got bored very fast."

Mary and her husband, Jim, who both come from the San Francisco area, lived in Des Moines, Iowa, before they came to Las Vegas. The couple had split up several times, and in 1972 Mary left Jim and took their sons to Phoenix, where she moved in with an aunt and uncle. "Then Jim arrived in Phoenix in our broken-down old Rambler"—she laughs—"and convinced me we should get back together and move home to San Francisco. So off we went. All he had brought with him was our pots and pans and some blankets and sheets. He had seventy-five dollars in his pocket—and that was it!"

On their way to San Francisco the Flatts drove through Las Vegas and decided to stop for a while. A friend of Jim's stayed with a girl friend so the family could have his apartment while Jim went job-hunting. Once he got a job at one of the casinos, and received his first paycheck, the Flatts got their own apartment.

"For the first two months we didn't have any furniture," Mary recalls, "so we slept on the floors. When people tell me their hard-luck stories, I tell them what we went through, and they stop bellyaching. They realize that we've been there too."

Mary's first job in Las Vegas was working as rental agent at the apartment building they lived in. She found it a nerve-racking occupation. "In this town," she explains "they're quick to put lock boxes on the tenants' doors when the rent is past due. Twice I had guns pulled on me by angry renters. There were other things, too. Two of my neighbors were hookers, and that was difficult for me to handle. You see, Vegas is a very different place to live in, and I was terribly naïve when I first got here. I finally quit the rental-agent job because I was becoming a nervous wreck."

Jim eventually got a job as a dealer at the craps tables at the MGM Hotel casino, while Mary took whatever work she could find, which sometimes included waiting tables at local places. Among other things, she tried selling Liquid Embroidery and being an Avon lady. "But I would get bored and quit," she admits, "I knew I couldn't be content as a homemaker, but I just couldn't find a job I could stick with for more than a few months. I was terribly frustrated, but I was determined to find something. I just didn't know what it was that I was looking for, that's all."

Mary was vacationing in San Francisco when she saw what she was looking for. "I was at a party I didn't even want to go to," she recalls, "and a messenger came to deliver a singing telegram. It was a straight, very serious song—a typical Western Union song! Well, it struck me that it was very unusual and outrageous to have a thing like this happen, but nobody laughed at all—including me. But right then and there I envisioned how much fun singing telegrams could be, and I said to myself, 'I'm taking this back to Vegas!' " The whole event was so important to Mary that she remembers the date—March 15, 1976.

"I didn't tell anyone about my idea, though," she says. "I didn't need any discouragement from my family and friends, and I knew they'd do their best to talk me out of it." Mary didn't even mention the idea at first to her parents, because she knew they would have a negative reaction too. But on April 1, 1976, she received her business license. "April Fool's Day was an appropriate time, don't you think?" she says with a mischievous grin.

Although Jim is now working full-time in Eastern Onion, he was totally against the idea in the beginning. "First of all," Mary says, shaking her head, "he thought the whole idea was nuts, just crazy. And second, he had seen me go through so many jobs and never last more than a few months. When I sold Avon and Liquid Embroidery, he watched me buy sales kits and then not stick with that either. So he figured it was just a matter of time until I was out of this, too. He kept telling me. 'You're crazy. You're absolutely nuts!' He gave me zero support."

The family had no cash that could be used to start the business, but Mary knew there would be investment in costumes, songs, and messengers' salaries, and she was determined to find the money. "I had a sixty-four Continental that was in perfect condition, and I just loved it," she continues. "But I had to sell it for seven hundred dollars, because I needed the money to start the business.

"I estimated that I'd need an additional five hundred to get the business going, and I racked my brains trying to think of somebody who could lend it to me. Finally I thought of my old high-school girl friend, Nita, who had married Andy Messerschmidt, the star pitcher for the Los Angeles Dodgers. 'Gosh,' I thought, 'I haven't seen her in years. How could I ask her for money?' I thought and thought about it, and I must have started dialing her number a hundred times and changed my mind. Finally I just said to myself, 'Well, the worst thing she can do is say no, and then I'm no worse off than I am right now,' so I called her. I still don't know what I would have done if she'd turned me down.

"When Nita answered, I just said, 'Nita, this is Mary Flatt, and I'm starting a new business and I need five hundred dollars.' And she said, 'Okay.' She never questioned me, and the money arrived in two days. I was ecstatic. I couldn't believe anyone could be so terrific.

"That five hundred was all the money in the world to me at the time. I was so busted I couldn't have paid my telephone bill without that money. It took me a year and a half to pay Nita back. I was really embarrassed because I couldn't pay her sooner, and I kept calling to tell her, 'Nita, I haven't forgotten.' I'd send her fifty dollars here and there—that was all I could afford. When I finally paid the loan off, I gave her some extra money to cover the interest, and she didn't even want to accept it. I had to insist. She was just terrific about the whole thing!"

Mary began her singing-telegram venture working at a makeshift desk in her home, and without a car. "My girl friends would call me up and say, 'Mary, I've got to go out of town. Would you baby-sit my car?' And everybody offered to drive me around to do my errands. But I have to admit that there were days when I felt absolutely stranded without a car. I mean, there were days when I couldn't even get outside my house. It was very frustrating and discouraging—but I had to prove to my friends and family, and to myself, that I could do it, so I wouldn't give up."

Despite their helpfulness, Mary's friends were not convinced the business would work. "Everybody had their *ifs, ands,* and *buts,*" she says. "There wasn't anybody who was supportive—including Jim. He was still convinced this was one of my flaky ideas, and I wasn't going to stick with it. Of course, with the work history I had, who could blame him for thinking like that? But I knew I had to get rid of all those fears and doubts, so I completely shut those thoughts out of my mind."

Once Mary had ordered her business cards and received her business license, her next step was to hire some messengers. "I didn't even have a song written! I was determined, but I really applied absolutely no common sense whatsoever." The next thing Mary did was place a one-dollar ad for messengers in a small local newspaper called *The Nifty Nickel*. The ad brought her one of Eastern Onion's best assets—Paul Terry.

"Paul was the first applicant that came through the door, and he was out of a job. He was just a kid in his early twenties, and I knew absolutely nothing about him. Anyway, I told him I was hiring some singing messengers, and he asked to see the songs. I explained that I needed some songs that would be very funny, and a little bit on the morbid side—dry humor, where people could laugh at their sickness, divorce, or their birthday when they were getting older. Then I told him that to qualify for the job he had to write me a song!

"Paul's a genius," Mary says, beaming. "In no time flat he came up with our birthday song, our first song, which is still our most popular one. It goes:

> We're marching closer to the grave,
> Wrinkles 'most everywhere.

Your mind and body will crumble,
You'll lose your teeth and your hair.
So while you're young enjoy the fun,
'Cause it's your birthday.

Not only did Paul get the job, but he became the official Eastern Onion songwriter."

Three applicants answered that first ad, and Mary hired all three. A woman who had helped Mary make her clothes produced the first Eastern Onion costumes. Later, as new songs were needed, Paul wrote them on demand. Today Eastern Onion has a repertoire of ninety-six songs—thirty were written by Paul Terry, who is no longer with the company.

Mary laughs, remembering the demands she made on Paul in those early days. "An order would come in and we'd say, 'Yes, we have an anniversary song,' or whatever it was, and we'd schedule it. Then I'd frantically call Paul and tell him to write me a song. I just wouldn't put up with any excuses, either—I wanted that song! Thank goodness Paul's a fantastic songwriter and a wonderful human being, or he would have told me where to get off a long time ago!

"Paul also has a great sense of humor. He can do as many fake voices as Rich Little, and he's terrific. Someday he's going to be a major show-business personality. Well, one day he called me on the telephone and put on a fake voice and pretended to be an eccentric millionaire. He said he was getting his dog spayed, and he wanted a song for her. Naturally, I wasn't about to turn down *any* business, so I just went on and on and told him we'd do it, and wrote the invoice up.

"Paul carried this on for five minutes before he broke up laughing and told me who it was. He said, 'I don't believe you, Mary. I suppose you were going to call me up and say that you wanted me to write a dog-spaying song in five minutes!'

"I said, 'Of course. Where else would I get one?'

"But that was great, because that was when we got the idea of having a no-occasion song. Now it's one of our most popular. We've delivered it in restaurants, at parties, even at the office, wherever the customer can gather a lot of people."

Mary emphasizes the importance of always obtaining the permission of whoever is in charge when a gram is delivered to a public place, such as an office building, restaurant, hotel lobby, or casino. "Otherwise, when the messenger comes on like gangbusters, he might get somebody like a maître d' or head nurse very upset," she explains. "Just imagine our messenger coming in dressed in costume and blowing the siren whistle and shouting for the recipient. 'Paula, Paula! I'm looking for Paula! I've got a message for you, sweetheart. It's from Michael! He says I should tell you. . . .' And then the messenger goes into the no-occasion song, with the monkey clapping the cymbals and everything.

> Oh no, it's not your happy birthday,
> Nor your anniversary.
> Oh no, it isn't April Fool's Day,
> Or your granny's pregnancy.
> It's just a song from good old Mike
> To lighten up the atmosphere,
> And make you feel *ridiculous*,
> In front of everybody here.

"Then he may play a little kazoo solo.

> Yes, I'm the guy from Eastern Onion,
> I'll sing a song in your behalf.
> And then we hope you'll die laughing
> So that on your epitaph
> It'll read, 'Here lies poor old Paula,
> Whose heart just didn't last,'
> And beneath your name your biggest claim to fame
> Was that you died a horse's ass."

The fees for a standard Eastern Onion act begin at twenty-eight dollars but can go as high as $150 for a Harem Gram, featuring a singing messenger and three belly dancers—a fifteen-minute show guaranteed to wow the most jaded partygoer. Like every gram, this one will be remembered far longer than a dozen roses or a couple of new ties. Then, too, a gram is always delivered in the presence of a group, so many people enjoy this unusual gift, not just the recipient.

Grams are funny, showy, and a little risqué, and the Eastern Onion messenger does not just come through the door—typically, he or she bursts on the scene. The average recipient (who is often the target of some good-natured kidding in the song) is not very articulate about his or her reaction. "Um, I'm flabbergasted," may be the initial comment. Just about everyone agrees, however, that getting a gram sure beats blowing out candles. Not only does the messenger do a brief song and dance, but he or she also delivers a handwritten pink telegram, and often a gag gift, purchased through Eastern Onion for a nominal extra fee.

The first Eastern Onion act was a messenger in very fancy dress: a tuxedo with a red jacket and black top hat. The messenger also came equipped with a mechanical cymbal-clapping monkey strapped at the waist and with more music-making instruments, including a kazoo, a siren whistle, and a tambourine. Today many other grams have been added, including Country Onion (who wears a cowboy suit), Clown Onion, Super Onion Man, Super Onion Woman, Mae East, and Macho Man. And there's Super Chicken, the Gorilla Gram, and the popular Belly Gram.

Eastern Onion has grams to celebrate occasions nobody else has figured out how to celebrate—such as the Happy Divorce Gram. Like most Eastern Onion grams, this one is sung to an old, familiar tune—in this case, "Toot Toot Tootsie, Good-bye," with, of course, a kazoo solo at the end. In part, the lyrics go:

> Good-bye, marriage, good-bye,
> It's time to look for another guy.
> I'll pay the divorce fee,
> But will you please still do my laundry?
> Breaking up is seldom okay,
> But I try to see it this way:
> I'm not losing a wife, the kids' ol' ma,
> I'm gaining the good riddance of a mother-in-law. . . .

As the repertoire of songs and acts grew, so did business—after a slow start. The first week, Eastern Onion did a grand total of five grams at fifteen dollars each, of which the messenger received seven dollars. Mary relied on two things to build the business at first: word of mouth, and "comps." She borrowed the idea of comps from the casinos, where gambling customers are often attracted by complimentary meals, rooms, or tickets to nightclub acts. Mary believed that if people saw the singing telegrams in person they would realize how much fun they were.

"The comps really taught me something," the pretty brunette says ruefully. "You can't depend on your friends to help you when you start a business. I sent comps to all kinds of friends, and nobody I sent them to ever ordered a gram afterwards. Everybody I thought I could count on to help me never did. Never! But it was good for me, because I had to learn to stand on my own two feet and not depend on anybody.

"But at least I was getting the messengers out, and they needed the experience. And the people who were there at the time of delivery would get excited about it. So, in effect, I was paying the messengers seven dollars to go out and advertise our service, and slowly, by word of mouth, we began to do business."

Mary's eyes dance as she tells about sending her husband a birthday gram a month or so after she started Eastern Onion. The messenger caught Jim between shifts in the crowded employees' lunchroom at the MGM Grand Hotel's casino. Like all Eastern Onion messengers, "The guy was a one-man band," Mary says happily. "He had the clapping monkey, the kazoo, the tambourine, the siren whistle. And, of course, almost nobody had ever seen our service; we were brand-new.

'Well, the guy went up to Jim's table and sang to him in front of about three hundred people. The whole joint got hysterical, while Jim sat there with sweat pouring down his arms, in a mild state of shock. He told me later he was just numb.

"When it was over, Jim called me up, and I was waiting. He's basically shy, and I knew he'd be upset! Sure, it was his birthday, but I also did it for the advertising, and he knew it. He carried on and told me he was so embarrassed he wanted to crawl under the table. But he also said he'd never had so much attention in his entire life. He said everybody there came up and patted him on the back and wished him a happy birthday—he'd *never* had so many people recognize his birthday. Well, he went on and on about the fuss they made, and all mixed in with it he was mad at me—*but he loved it!* He just didn't want to admit it.''

That day Jim also gave Mary the first advice he'd ever offered about the business: when Eastern Onion delivered a gram to a casino, it should always be cleared in advance. The advice turned out to be sound, and it is now Eastern Onion policy. Mary believes it essential for Eastern Onion franchises to establish good rapport with the people who have the power to veto singing telegrams: headwaiters, maître d's, and hotel managers, for instance. "It's standard procedure for us to let them know we're coming. Otherwise, you can just imagine how upset they might become. Just picture having a Gorilla Gram delivered at a fancy French restaurant without tipping off the maître d' first!"

Mary has always been concerned about establishing a good business reputation, and as a result all Eastern Onion franchises are well-respected enterprises in their communities. "One thing we learned very early," she points out, "was that a gram must be delivered on time. *Exactly* on time. If a messenger gets there five minutes early and the gift-giver isn't there to see him come in, he's going to be very upset. Customers often say to us, 'Look, we're not giving any other presents, you're it! We want to see the reaction, so be sure your messenger is there at seven-fifteen on the dot.' And we do make sure."

When a customer has any complaint at all, Mary insists on refunding the cost of the gram in full—even though she still has to pay the messenger. "But in the long run," she says, "this has paid off for us in terms of reputation. And about seventy-five percent of our business is repeats, too. That tells us something, doesn't it?"

Eastern Onion is an excellent example of the fact that even the best idea needs promotion to make it work. During the company's first ten months in business, it made barely enough to pay the bills—although Mary herself was working sixteen-hour days, and often seven days a week. "It was a real grind," she recalls, "and there were many times I thought about going back to work with a normal job that would give me a paycheck at the end of the week. I was beginning to think Eastern Onion was a ridiculous idea. And it didn't help any that everyone around me was telling me the same thing."

Then Mary hired Vaughan Ryan, a Las Vegas public-relations expert, who put her on radio and television. When she was invited to appear on several local shows, she was "absolutely petrified! I'd never been on the air, and I was so nervous I couldn't eat or sleep for two days before my first appearance. But somehow I got through it, and surprisingly, people told me I handled the whole thing rather well."

By this time, Mary had built the Las Vegas office to the point where it was doing about twenty grams a week. She first appeared on the air with the Eastern Onion gang the day before Valentine's Day. In the next twenty-four hours the company did *eighty* grams.

"We couldn't get over the results," Mary bubbles. "I had never actually made any money in the business until that day, although I had always believed Eastern Onion would someday be a winner. But now it was a reality—not just a dream I believed in. That one day made up for all the time and effort and sleepless nights. I knew we were going to make it. After that, nothing could stop me!"

In later years, the thrill of that first big Valentine's Day was not diminished for Mary by the discovery that Valentine's Day is the best day of the year for any Eastern Onion office. A typical office does a full week's work on that one day. The Chicago franchise, for instance, does five hundred grams a week, and five hundred grams on Valentine's Day alone. The first big Valentine's Day was not just an isolated moment of success. Once Eastern Onion was publicized, weekly grams began to climb, until the Las Vegas Eastern Onion now averaged a hundred grams a week.

While Eastern Onion is now becoming a household word across the nation, Mary had no idea when she started the company that it would ever become so successful. "I just wanted to *survive*," she says with an emphatic gesture. "I wanted to be able to pay the rent. Oh, sometimes I would dream that we might become a McDonald's someday, but I didn't ever take my dreams seriously."

Even when Eastern Onion became an established success in Las Vegas, it did not occur to Mary to think seriously about expanding to other cities until 1978. Then Jim Edmondson, a bartender who had seen numerous grams delivered, got more and more interested in the service. Finally he called Mary and asked, "Do you sell franchises?"

Although she never had, Mary immediately said, "Yes."

"I'd like to come over and buy one for Phoenix," he said.

"No problem," Mary told him.

She laughs when she recalls her confident reply. "We didn't even have a manual! As soon as I hung up, I called Paul and told him we had to make one. He's real good at that sort of thing, and the two of us started with the basics and put a manual together with everything in it, from songs to uniforms to our rate schedule. Jim Edmondson got a real bargain. We didn't know what to charge him, so I think it was something like three thousand dollars. And we gave him a five-year contract, charging him two percent of his gross. When that expires, he'll pay five percent like everyone else!"

Today the initial investment in an Eastern Onion franchise varies depending on the population of the city. A franchise in a major city will cost twenty thousand dollars or more. A typical franchise nets a 30 percent return on its annual volume; the Hawaii franchise made over one hundred thousand dollars in its first year. Eastern Onion franchises can become successful very quickly—the Detroit franchise grossed forty-five thousand dollars its second month in business.

Surprisingly, Mary did not register a trademark for the name "Eastern Onion" until after she sold the Phoenix franchise. At the same time she also applied for trademarks for such properties as the monkey, the songs, and the company logos. Why did she wait so long? It was simply a matter of not being able to afford the fees when the business was just getting established.

Once Eastern Onion franchises began to sell through word of mouth, Mary's husband, Jim, became interested. Eventually he quit his job at MGM to concentrate on franchise sales. For the first time in their marriage, the couple worked together effectively as a team.

"We still have our share of arguments," Mary admits, "but we've gotten along much better since we've been in business together. We've seen this happen with many of the other couples who have Eastern Onion franchises, too; our most successful operations are husband-wife teams."

In January 1977, with eight franchises sold and operating, the Flatts finally moved their offices out of their home to a building where they rented desk space from an answering-service business. The following year the company moved into its present location. Mary, Jim, and their two sons—who came to Las Vegas with seventy-five dollars—have since moved to a spacious ranch house fully equipped with a large swimming pool and hot tub. Jim now drives a brand-new Cadillac Seville, and Mary, who sold her car to start the business, has a van and a Thunderbird convertible.

The Las Vegas Eastern Onion offices, about 1,100 square feet, are on the second floor of a Strip shopping center with a beautiful view of Sunrise Mountain. The office is reminiscent of a real-estate office, with open space surrounded by eight desks on either side of the room. One wall holds the humorous gifts and toys which an Eastern Onion messenger will deliver along with the gram for an extra fee. These include such novelty items as T-shirts, Horny Toads, baby-doll "flashers," and other suggestive gifts. Yes-No Pillows, for instance, are just what the name implies. If a woman is "in the mood" she turns the Yes side up on her bed. The No side, as Mary explains it, means, "Not tonight dear, I have a headache." Next to Mary's desk hangs a large bulletin board with the names and work schedules of the Las Vegas messengers. One of the walls is decorated with musical notes, indicating the singing-telegram theme of the company.

Jim stands a trim five-foot-nine, with strawberry-blond hair, deep-blue eyes, and a healthy-looking tan. A soft-spoken man, he chooses his words carefully—quite a contrast from the effervescent Mary. Most of the time Jim wears very casual clothes accented with heavy gold chains around his neck.

He explains that every franchise is a turnkey operation patterned after the Las Vegas organization. "Mary worked very hard to get the kinks out of this business," he says in a northern California drawl. "There's no sense having each new franchise make the same mistakes Eastern Onion made in the beginning here. So that's one of the advantages of joining us. We offer a package that's guaranteed to be successful if it's followed to the letter—it doesn't make any difference where the franchise opens up. People are people, and they get a big kick out of our grams everywhere."

Mary interrupts, "Actually, Vegas is not a great town for this business, although at first blush you might think so. In fact, a lot of people felt we couldn't make it because there's already so much entertainment here—it's the entertainment capital of the world. There's probably more action with the nightclub acts going on here every night than in the rest of the country combined. So if we can get their attention here, we can anticipate doing even better in other cities."

In Las Vegas and other Eastern Onion cities, grams have been delivered in some unusual places. Freddie Prinz once received a gram onstage during his act. "It had been cleared first," Mary explains, "but *he* didn't know about it till the messenger ran onstage. He took it like a good sport. Of course," she adds thoughtfully, "he actually didn't have much choice, in front of an audience." One Las Vegas messenger, delivering a gram to a suite at Caesar's Palace, walked in on an orgy. The startled messenger, assured that he was in the right place, sang away to a roomful of amorous nude people. Grams have also been delivered to other entertainers—offstage—including Debbie Reynolds, the Bee Gees, Loretta Lynn, Tom Jones, Charlton Heston, Burt Reynolds, Ray Krock, and Wayne Newton.

For all its celebrity appeal, Eastern Onion seems to be popular with people of every age and economic background. While some customers are affluent, Mary notes that the bulk of the Las Vegas business comes from "Ordinary nine-to-five working people—people from all walks of life. I can't tell you how many grams we deliver to firemen, policemen, bartenders, waitresses, and secretaries. It's not unusual for several people in an office to pool their money and order a gram. I guess it's a heck of a way to liven up an otherwise dull afternoon! Anyway, if the boss is retiring, what would he be more likely to remember—a belly dancer shimmying up to him, or a retirement watch?"

While Eastern Onion has a universal appeal, it also has its share of sex appeal. Women messengers wear black fishnet stockings with black leotards and a little red vest. Other women messengers include a sexy French maid who delivers a sexy message. Male messengers include Superman and Macho Man, who will strip down to their G-strings. All messengers deliver gag gifts which can be quite suggestive—if that's what the customer orders. Eastern Onion's sexiness is all in good clean fun, and delivered with broad strokes of humor.

Through trial and error, Eastern Onion has learned to reject certain requests for telegrams which are too difficult to deliver. "The airports are terrible places to send a messenger," Mary states. "We've done it, but the planes often don't arrive on time, and it's very difficult to *find* people at an airport, so we rarely accept those requests. We do go to private parties, but we screen those carefully, so we're sure somebody will be there when the messenger arrives. And we turn down requests to do it one-to-one; if you go to someone's home and he's not expecting you, you might not get in the door! Anyway, it's boring. The more people are there, the more fun it is for everyone."

The Las Vegas Eastern Onion has sent messengers as far as San Diego by airplane on request, and other franchises have had similar assignments. All franchise contracts cover a sixty-mile radius, with an additional three-dollar fee for every ten miles. In Las Vegas, Eastern Onion is open twenty-four hours a day, every day, but most franchises close between midnight and two A.M.

Eastern Onion messengers are a special breed of people. Most are performers waiting for a chance to break into show business. As Mary explains, a messenger has to have a strong desire to be in the limelight, so that delivering grams is something he or she loves and would be willing to do for nothing. Good messengers earn from a hundred to five hundred dollars a week, depending on their schedules, with much of this income derived from the tips given by pleased onlookers when a gram is delivered. It is not difficult to attract potential messengers with an Eastern Onion ad, but out of twenty who may respond to an ad, only two or three will audition well enough to be considered.

Not only do Eastern Onion messengers have to be talented, they must be extroverted and flexible. "There's nothing bashful about our messengers," Mary says happily. "And they just adjust to anything. You know, a messenger can be in McDonald's for a gram, and a half-hour later be over at Caesar's Palace in the plush Bacchanal Room. That requires a very special type of person.

"Anyway, it takes a real ham to burst into a roomful of people and shout at the top of his voice, 'Eastern Onion singing telegram for Jeanne.' The messenger is then led to the table, shouting and blowing his siren whistle. Let's face it, that's something not everyone can do!"

Mary herself has never delivered a gram, despite the repeated urgings of the messengers. "I just haven't been able to muster up the nerve," she admits. "In fact, I have really gone out of my way to avoid it. The closest I ever got was when I didn't have anyone to do a gram at a bank. Well, I went to the apartment of my girl friend who's a singer at one of the casinos, and I literally got her out of bed, dressed her, coached her, sang to her all the way, and made her do it. It would have been less trouble to do it myself, I'm sure. But I just don't have the confidence to be in entertainment."

Messengers confront some unusual situations when delivering grams. The New York franchise, for instance, got a request from a shy customer to deliver an "I love you" to his girl friend in Central Park. The customer escorted the messenger to the right spot, pointed out his girl friend, and then hid behind a tree while the messenger sang. At the end of the gram, the messenger handed the woman an envelope, as instructed, in which was a proposal of marriage.

"Just tell him I accept," she told the messenger, at which point the young man came out from behind the tree—at last—and embraced her.

Another customer ordered a messenger dressed in a baby's dress, including ruffled tennis panties, and outfitted with a baby bottle, a rattle, and a pacifier. The messenger was cleared to enter a sales meeting at a large corporation and sing to the customer's husband. The polite congratulations song informed the executive that his wife was pregnant! The somewhat dazed messenger reported that the man nearly fainted on the spot.

Because the messengers represent the service Eastern Onion is selling, they are rigorously critiqued on an ongoing basis. The critique manager spot-checks grams as they are delivered, and checks off the performance against a list. The messenger is graded on such aspects as appearance, projection, and memorization of songs, on a scale from one to ten. In Eastern Onion, this critiquing supplies the quality control over the service.

The critique manager also notes whether a messenger passes out Eastern Onion business cards to everyone at the conclusion of the gram. "If someone fails to do this," Mary says, "he's fired on the spot! After all, we generate most of our new business by word of mouth from people who see a delivery. It would be a terrible waste for someone to call another service because our messenger didn't pass out our business cards!"

The Eastern Onion training program for messengers includes video training tapes and plenty of live performance on comps, so the trainees get over their initial stage fright. The friends who get these comps also critique the messengers, who do this without pay as part of their training.

These and more Eastern Onion practices have all been codified as the franchising end of the business has grown. The manual tells the franchisee, chapter and verse, how to open in a city with a splash. It includes a standard format for radio, television, and newspaper advertising, and suggestions for generating interest. For instance, a new franchise may trade grams for publicity and commercial spots on local radio and television stations. New franchises also follow Mary's successful format in using comps at the beginning; the manual spells out whom to give them to and exactly how. Songs, acts, costumes, accounting and operational procedures—every aspect of the business is detailed. The heavy manual itself is copyrighted, and every franchisee is warned that if it is lost, there is a thousand-dollar replacement cost.

"It's a *wonderful* system," Mary bubbles. "We can have a new franchise generating profits in a matter of weeks. This is the *only* business I know of where a franchisee can get his money back within six months. Suppose he invests eighty thousand dollars, between our fee and the costumes and everything. In six months he will have that eighty-thousand back and he'll be making a profit."

Recently an Eastern Onion Owners' Association was formed, which operates on a small scale in a fashion similar to that of the McDonald's Owners' Association. Each franchisee pays the association a hundred-dollar monthly fee and a percentage of his monthly volume, which goes into a national advertising fund. The association also holds national conventions of all Eastern Onion franchise owners. Mary's brown eyes light up when she talks about the latest convention. "We've got an unbelievable group of owners. And it was so great to exchange ideas and see everyone share the responsibility. Many heads are so much better than one."

Five of the present Eastern Onion franchise owners are former Las Vegas casino people who saw the service in action, much as Jim Edmondson did. One of these, Nelson Fernandez, is widely admired for the success of the Miami franchise. "But when he went into it," Mary says breathlessly, "people were shocked! He was walking away from a very prominent position as a baccarat boss at the Sands. But he knew what he was doing, and he's a shrewd businessman. Today he's making more than ever. But I don't think that matters to him as much as the fact that he's enjoying a better life-style now. He's living where he wants to and doing what he wants to do. Working in a casino can take a lot out of you over a period of time."

While some franchisees were previously entrepreneurs, others include a former attorney, a builder, and a restaurant manager. "We've been selective in selling franchises," Mary says, "and it's paid off, for them and for us."

There's no question that Mary Flatt's "crazy" idea has paid off. Everyone associated with Eastern Onion is making money, and having a grand time doing it. And most of all, the customers love it. Eastern Onion seems to be here to stay. So don't be surprised if someday, when you least expect it, a gorilla, a chicken, a belly dancer, or even Superman pays you a call. If it isn't a bird and it isn't a plane, it must be Eastern Onion!

7

Rent-a-Wreck®

Wearing well-worn jeans, running shoes, and a T-shirt, he sports a full red beard. A frayed baseball cap sits on his bushy reddish hair. The quizzical expression on his face reminds you a little of a middle-aged, larger-than-life Woody Allen; in fact, so does his accent and his way of moving from one thought to another in an unbroken stream. The little office building he is standing in is surrounded by a jumble of cars, and within easy hearing of the Santa Monica Freeway overpass a stone's throw away. Obviously used to the noise, he strokes the large gray cat cradled in his left arm. The cat has the same contented air of its master.

Would you rent a used car from this man?

If you're in the majority of people who rent used cars, you probably would, because you've just met Dave Schwartz, founder and chairman of the board of Rent-a-Wreck, the world's largest used-car rental agency, and one of America's fastest-growing franchise operations.

Just as Dave is an unlikely candidate for the role of successful entrepreneur, his Rent-a-Wreck agency does not look like the thriving enterprise that it is. Its location on busy Pico Boulevard in a light-industry section of West Los Angeles is convenient, but unglamorous. The lot is crowded with cars of all ages, some late-model, some very old, some slightly dented or scratched here or there. It looks like what it once was—a typical used-car lot—but there are no "For Sale" signs on these vehicles. They represent part of Dave's overflowing rental inventory. And this is only one of nearly 150 Rent-a-Wreck locations.

Dave's entrepreneurial instincts actually surfaced quite early in life. When he was only ten years old, he set up a paying craps game in his house with a set his parents had brought back from Las Vegas. When he was fifteen he had his own Christmas-tree lot. His first business transaction with an automobile occurred a year later, when he paid three hundred dollars for a 1941 Ford. He smiles at the recollection. "My idea of bargaining with the used-car guy was to say, 'I don't suppose you'd take any less, would you?' Of course he said no." Dave believes he valued his car more because his father insisted that he pay for it himself.

As an art major at UCLA, Dave sold real estate for a short time. "I looked so young, nobody wanted to buy from me, but I did get a good education in real estate." After that, he worked his way through school by buying his friends' used cars for the trade-in value and reselling them at a profit. He also bought twenty-five-dollar junkers for an automobile-wrecking yard, earning two dollars for each car he brought in. Between selling perhaps five junkers a day and reselling his friends' used cars, Dave earned comfortable money for a college student. More important, he had drifted into the automobile business.

In 1959, when he graduated from UCLA, Dave had two assets: an M.A. in English and theater arts, and an accumulation of cars he had not resold. He decided that the used-car business would be more rewarding than a teaching career, and leased his first used-car lot from a friend in exchange for Dave's spending the necessary two thousand dollars to level the lot. Dave named the business, which was located on Bundy Street and Pico Boulevard, Bundy Used Cars.

When Dave was twenty-four, he moved to a larger lot, across the street from his present location. The following year it was announced that the Santa Monica Freeway was coming through; he would have to move again. As he was searching for a new location, a neighboring businessman came to him with an offer he couldn't refuse. The businessman, who was having serious financial problems, owned the entire city block across the street from Dave. The offer was simple: buy the whole block for no money down. The only capital outlay would be four thousand dollars for back taxes so that the title could be transferred. The hitch was that the block was worth about $110,000 and the owner was asking $130,000, which was what he needed to clear his debt on the property.

Dave's first move was to talk to people who knew more about real estate than he did. "Every one of them told me the same thing," he recalls. " 'Don't buy it. You'd be crazy to overpay like that.' "

Dave smiles. "They knew more than I did about real estate, but the deal still made sense to me. It didn't require any money down; I'd have my own lot and couldn't be kicked out when the lease expired; I had to move anyway and—wow!—to own a whole city block at age twenty-five!" Reasoning that the property would someday increase in value, Dave went ahead and made the deal. As it turned out, it was years before California real estate began to appreciate, but today the property is worth millions of dollars.

Dave borrowed a thousand dollars from his mother to add to his used-car inventory, and Bundy Used Cars found a new location. Two years later, in addition to his mortgage, Dave was in debt to various creditors for approximately a hundred thousand dollars. "I actually lost that much money by poor business management," he marvels. "So by the time I was twenty-seven I had built up this huge negative net worth.

"I tried borrowing money from banks. Every time I went, I'd put on my coat and tie, get myself all psyched up to give them a great presentation—and they'd turn me down. Finally I analyzed it and concluded that it was because I wasn't being me. It made me come across nervous. So I said, 'To hell with it,' and started going to banks dressed like I do now, clean, but in old clothes, maybe with a hole in my tennis shoes. And you know what? I never got turned down after that, never ever. Because I was talking from the gut instead of the throat. *I* had confidence in me, so *they* had confidence in me.

"I've had the same banker for seventeen years now, and we laugh about it sometimes. Whenever I needed ten or fifteen thousand dollars he'd loan it to me. They used to get mad at him, but he was willing to take chances because he believed in me."

When Dave went after loans in Levi's and tennis shoes, he did not have the gray-streaked red beard he wears today. "It's a 'flu beard,' " he explains. "I had the flu this year, and I was too lazy to shave. Then I sort of liked this, so I decided to keep it. I had a mustache back then, though. Actually, I haven't shaved in five years. I hate to shave, *hate* it, so every Saturday morning at seven I used to stop by my barber's on the way to work, and he'd shave me."

After Dave assessed his stunning negative net worth at age twenty-seven, he decided it was time to change the way he did business. Instead of selling cars for high prices and low down payments, he would sell them very inexpensively, cash only. Knowing how to buy cars cheaply, he could afford to sell them at low prices. "And let's face it," he says, shaking his head, "I'm not a bill collector. Chasing people down was a lot of negative energy."

By this point in his career, Dave had already developed a selling philosophy that would serve him well in later years. "I'd tell people, 'Now, this car drives real well now, but after you go about twenty miles, the transmission slips a little.' Or I'd tell them, 'You're going to need a new battery.' I'd let them know exactly what was wrong with the car.

"Unlike other car dealers, I didn't accentuate the positive to get someone to buy. I admitted the car's faults up front. If the car turned out to be in better condition than I said, nobody's disappointed." This approach was so successful that Dave carried it to its logical extreme and changed his sign to read "Bundy's Very Used Cars." Occasionally someone would ask him "How do you have the nerve to sell these wrecks?" Dave would respond truthfully, "Yeah, these are just old cars," or "Hey, you're not in a Cadillac agency."

Dave thinks that used-car dealers who try to pass off their cars as new are making a mistake. "They're not taking advantage of the fact that they *are* used. That's my negative sell, and it works."

Business began to prosper with Dave's new approach. "I was an inventive businessman," he says straightforwardly, "for a kid, anyway. I wasn't afraid to work, and I wasn't afraid to take chances. And I enjoyed my work.'' By 1969 he had accumulated a good inventory of cars, as well as additional property. Then he met his second reversal when a friend who was a broker urged him to invest in some stock. Six months later, it seemed like the best thing he'd ever done; he realized a profit of seven thousand dollars on his small investment.

"I never could accumulate a lot of cash," he explains, "so when that happened I thought, 'Geez, I work seven days a week, and here I can make all this money without doing *anything.*' So I went to the banks and borrowed on everything I could, bought stock, borrowed on the stock, and bought more stock. Then *boom, boom, boom,* the stocks went down to practically nothing! I owed so much money it was a joke. Here I am, thirty-three years old, and I'm in debt for like a quarter of a million dollars! I had hocked everything. I had leveraged every way I could to borrow so I could buy more and more stock. And once you get into debt, and you've got some loans, it's always easier to borrow more."

As everyone Dave knew told him, the solution was obvious— bankruptcy. But he had owned the property the lot sat on for eight years now; it had not appreciated much yet, but he was certain it would. He cast about for another answer.

"Now, right during this time, a young woman came in and bought a car from me for ninety-five dollars. It broke down the same day, and she called to tell me about it. Everybody else would either give the customer another car or a hard time. I just said, ''I'll give you back your money.' I always did this kind of thing, because I can see the fifty-cent piece behind the dime. Give her back the ninety-five dollars and she's going to tell a hundred people about it. But that's not the only reason. She was a nice girl, and I didn't want to stick her. You can't grind everyone, that's all.

"So when I told her I'd give her back her money, she said, 'That's nice of you, but I really need a car. I'll be out here three months, and I have $225. Could you rent me a car for three months?'

"I said, 'I'd like to, but I can't. I don't have the insurance.'

"So she suggested that I sell her the car for $225, so she could assume responsibility for liability insurance, and in three months she'd bring it back and sell it to me for one dollar. Well, it was her idea, and I didn't want to go through all that paperwork, but I did it. I thought, 'What the heck . . .' Three months later she came in with the car. She said, 'Dave, God bless you. That was the best deal I ever made in my life. I don't know what to say, but *thank you!*' "

Dave slowly shakes his head and smiles. "I thought, 'This has to be the greatest deal I ever had. I got the money, I got back the car, she's happy, I'm happy. What's better than that?' "

Dave realized that most people would not want to go through that kind of paperwork to rent a car for a month or two, and he wanted to design his rental-car business to run as smoothly as possible. "I'm a very, very, very slow, lazy businessman," he says. "Really, I'm into *no grief,* and I want everything done right. I don't like to have to redo anything. I want everything clean and easy." He finally decided to take the first step and get rental-liability insurance; the cars were so cheap that he would pay any collision damages himself.

Next he went looking for an education. "Now, I wasn't the first person to rent used cars. I found a guy who had been doing it for a while and was going out of business, and asked him if he would help me. He said, 'Listen, I'll help you. You can call me twenty times a day if you want. But I'm telling you, it's the world's toughest business.' "

Dave's education in used-car rental turned out to be mainly trial and error after all, for his source had very few answers. "During the first six months I must have called him ten times a day. I supposed he'd learned about fifteen percent of the business, because that's how many of my questions he had answers for."

At the same time, Dave attempted to raise money to buy an inventory of rental cars. "I knew it could work. If I could buy a lot of cars and rent them, I could pay back my debts and have a business." After contacting seventy-five businessmen, he gave up. Despite his offer to give a backer a piece of the business, Dave could not raise capital. Moreover, without exception, everyone he talked to gave him the same advice: go bankrupt.

"They'd say, 'What, are you crazy? Who would rent a used car? It's insane. Just declare bankruptcy, start all over.'

"Go bankrupt, I thought, and lose all my property? I *know* I can make it back." For the nest two years, Dave worked sixteen hours a day, seven days a week. He sold cars and rented a few, pulling one car at a time out of his used-car inventory and putting it into the rental business. The one car became five, and then eleven. When the rental inventory hit twenty, Dave was elated.

Meanwhile, he got together with his creditors and worked out the lowest possible payments. Although they were still high, he managed to meet them, and slowly made inroads on his massive debt. After he advertised in *The Los Angeles Times*, he was contacted by a rabbi who agreed to loan him money on his property, despite the fact that it was already mortgaged for fifty thousand dollars more than it was worth.

To build the used-car rental business, Dave bought the smallest display ads available and advertised, "Rent a Used Car—Low Rates." (It has always been his policy not to advertise prices.) He went around to body shops and garages, asking them to send him customers whose cars were being repaired. And he kept putting one more car at a time in the rental inventory.

"And then," he says, "with one thing and another I had to sell off the rental cars, and the inventory was back down to four. I said, 'Oh, no, it's over. It's a bath.' But I kept on plugging away." One thing that kept him going was his sense of moral obligation to the banker who had believed in him. "That's the most important thing," he says. "I didn't stiff my banker."

He began again with the process of slowly building the inventory, and Bundy Used Car Rental began to attract more customers, most through word of mouth. By 1973, after four years of untiring work, Dave had turned the corner. The creditors were paid off, and he was still the sole owner of both his property and his business. As it turned out, being unable to get a backer was the best thing that ever happened to him.

"If someone had backed me," he says "I don't think I would have made it. I would have started with too many cars, and I wouldn't have been able to work into the business. This way I built on a solid foundation."

A large segment of Dave's clientele now came from the film

industry, a relatively small, close-knit community within which word travels fast. Some of his customers were unknown then; some were already stars. "It became chic to rent a car from me," he says. "Sort of reverse snobbism, maybe. Anyway, a lot of these people own Alphas or Mercedes, and they're always breaking down. So they need a rental while theirs is in the shop."

Dave's regular customers include director Francois Truffaut, Robin Williams of *Mork and Mindy*, and Linda Lavin, star of *Alice*, who rented a car for four years. Henry Fonda, who does all his own gardening, rents a '63 Chevy pickup truck several days each month. Other regulars are Alan Alda, Woody Allen, Ali MacGraw, Sarah Miles, Paul Newman, Phil Donahue, Ringo Starr, Connie Stevens, Ed Asner, Lily Tomlin, John Belushi and Dan Ackroyd, and Elton John.

Nobody gets preferential treatment from Dave Schwartz, no matter how famous. One customer called Dave recently and asked, "Was that Ali MacGraw behind me in line when I was in the other day?" Dave assured him it was.

Dave does have a way of paying special tribute to some customers, however, by naming cars in their honor. Howard Koch, who wrote *Casablanca*, regularly rents a light-blue 1969 Pontiac LeMans. Dave is fond of the movie, and remembered that across the street from Joe's Café, where much of the film's action takes place, is a bar called the Blue Parrot. As a result, the blue LeMans is now known on the lot as the Blue Parrot.

Somebody once described Dave as a casting director, and in a sense, there's truth to that statement. When the producer of *Family* was unable to convince Henry Fonda to star in the Christmas show, he happened to mention it to Dave. A few days later when Fonda came in to rent his truck, Dave mentioned to him that a friend of his had written a great script for that show. Fonda ended up taking the part. Brooke Adams was answering the phones at Rent-a-Wreck one day when Terry Malick, the director, came in to rent a car. As a result of their meeting there, Brooke got a part in the movie *Days of Heaven*.

Dave jokes that even the car you rent may have had a role in a movie the week before. Rent-a-Wreck is a well-known source in the industry for the older cars often needed to set the scene in films.

While many stars frequent Rent-a-Wreck, Dave sums up his typical customer as "an ordinary guy who feels secure with his life, star or no star. The more secure a person is, the kookier he can be. He doesn't care about his image. Now, the insecure person who's worried about what people think, we don't appeal to that kind of guy."

Dave has a soft spot for the law students from the major universities who come to Los Angeles each summer to clerk at large law firms. "Our customers are supposed to be twenty-five years old and have a major credit card, but we sort of relax our standards for them. We've never had a single problem with them."

Rent-a-Wreck cars are rented by the day, week, or month. The typical weekly rate is seventy-five to ninety dollars, with the first five hundred miles of driving free, and the customer buying his own gas. While some people drive Dave's older cars as reverse status symbols, others choose Rent-a-Wreck for the economy. Some customers are 'in limbo' between cars. Others have cars in the shop. Some want good, basic transportation while in town on vacation. Others want the nostalgia of driving a Mustang convertible, a VW bug, or some other 'classic' of their youth.

"You get executives," Dave says, smiling, "who rent from Hertz or Avis when they're on company time. But when they're in L.A. with the family on vacation, traveling 'on their own nickels,' they want to save money." Dave's premise is simple: almost everyone drives a used car at home; so why not drive a used car while you're traveling? "As a matter of fact, the cars you rent from the majors are used, too—ours are just slightly more used, that's all."

Dave shares with his customers a desire to get value for his money. He feels this is characteristic of the times, and helps account for Rent-a-Wreck's success. Recently, when he took his son to Europe, they flew over on the Concorde, for the experience. Coming back, however, they flew TWA standby. Dave, a multimillionaire in blue jeans, says earnestly, "It's not a matter of how much I could afford—I want value for my money. And I believe that's how most people think today.

"That's not how they used to think. Years ago, when I went to Hawaii, I rented a car from Budget for thirty-seven dollars for four days, and unlimited mileage. Well, I ran into an older couple at the hotel who were renting a Hertz for something like twenty-four dollars a day and twenty-four cents a mile. I asked them why they didn't go to Budget, and they said, 'Oh, we wouldn't take any off-brands!'

"Off-brands? We'd both rented the same kind of car! I don't believe people think like that today."

Another reason for Dave's success is the balance of economy and quality Rent-a-Wreck offers. While the major rental companies often seem most concerned with cleaning out the ashtrays and checking for scratches, those items are far down on Rent-a-Wreck's maintenance checklist. Every car is checked for wear on the brakes and tires, and for how well it runs. The Los Angeles agency employs three full-time mechanics for lot maintenance and road calls.

People who rent from Rent-a-Wreck tend to have different priorities than people who rent from the major companies. Dave explains, "When one of our customers gets a car with a lighter that doesn't work, he won't complain about it. He'll just go around telling everyone how well the car ran. If that happened with a car from one of the majors, he'd be griping his head off."

Dave's Mustang convertibles are a special source of pride. He purchased many of them for under a thousand dollars. Now they are worth over five thousand each. In buying cars, however, Dave does not look for investment, but for the cars he knows are dependable, easy to maintain, and in demand by customers. Medium-sized six-cylinder cars have steadily gained in popularity in recent years, as customers became more conscious of gas efficiency. Dave notes that even large corporations have become economy-minded in recent years and often send executives to Rent-a-Wreck instead of a major company.

Just as Rent-a-Wreck's customers are concerned about good value, Dave's concern as a businessman is simple: "return on investment." He points out a pathetic, battered Volkswagen bug which has taken in nearly thirty thousand dollars in rentals since 1972. "And runs perfect," he proclaims, stooping to scratch his dog, who has just wandered over. "I can buy a good low-mileage used car for under $1,500 that will pay for itself in rentals in a few months. It'll give me gross revenues of over $350 a month. *And* I have an asset that is actually appreciating in value."

The dog, a brush-tailed mix of dachshund and German shepherd, takes off, followed by the gray cat. "Oh, that cat's so smart," Dave says, business forgotten.

Dave Schwartz is a curious mixture, part hardheaded businessman and part unruffled, intuitive animal-lover. The intuition has come to play a major part in his business; it is something he tries to develop in franchisees who come to Los Angeles for training. His premise is simple: "The *right* customer will take good care of your car, keep your insurance rates down, and . . . he won't stick you." How do you tell the "right" customer? Over the years, Dave has learned to do it on the telephone as well as in person. He gives an example: 'When a guy calls and says very friendly, 'Hey, how ya doin'?' that guy's no good. Or suppose someone says very fast, very heavy-handed, 'What's your newest, cleanest, cheapest car?' Then I'm on the alert.

"Usually I'll say, 'When do you need it?'

"He'll invariably say, 'Right now.'

" 'Geez, I'm sorry, but we're booked.' "

Dave is at a loss to explain why certain types of people can be counted on to damage cars or lose them altogether. "There are just some things I've learned from experience. I know when a guy's a deadbeat; in fifteen seconds I know. If I trust them, I rent to them. It's as simple as that."

Dave's intuition gives rise to another mysterious ability—to pick out the right car for the customer moments after meeting him. This too was learned with time and experience. It is Dave's policy to give a customer a choice of only three cars—"More is a waste of time." Sometimes, however, he picks out just one, and when he does, it is almost always just what the customer would have ordered. Back when Rent-a-Wreck was still Bundy's Very Used Cars, this uncanny ability led directly to one of the biggest breaks Dave Schwartz ever had.

A visiting New Yorker, who happened to be a writer, came to the lot to rent a car. With sure instinct, Dave picked out a 1970 LeMans, and said, "If you don't like it, we'll give you something else." The customer loved it. But more than that, he was impressed by Dave's ability to fit the car to the customer so quickly and precisely. That evening he mentioned it at a party and found that eight other people there had rented from Dave Schwartz, and were equally fascinated by his intuition. The writer's article, "Zen and the Art of Car Rental," appeared some months later in the April 1975 issue of *New Times* magazine. Dave, whose biggest publicity heretofore had been two lines in *The Los Angeles Times,* was overwhelmed. He was also delighted by "one of my all-time favorite lines about my business: 'These cars are so old they still get Tokyo Rose on the radio.' "

The article contained a far more significant line, however: "Some people call them Rent-a-Wreck." His expression as complacent as that of the gray cat, who is back on his lap, Dave pushes back his baseball cap and talks about what happened next.

"After that, business was terrific. I've got a couple of hundred cars out, I'm making a lot of money, and I've paid back all my loans. I'm happy. Very happy, and I don't even want more business. So one hot Friday afternoon about four o'clock, I'd had a tough day, and I decided, 'Okay, I'm going to eliminate ninety-five percent of the people who come in.' I figured all I needed was my regulars and referrals. So I called up a sign painter and told him to change the name to Rent-a-Wreck. I figured ninety-five percent of the people who saw that would keep right on going.

"Well, it had the opposite effect. Maybe five percent of them hate the name. And ninety-five percent *love* it."

Not long after that, a customer came in on a Saturday afternoon, furious at a major rental company which advertised a certain car at a particular price but didn't have it available when he got there. On principle he had refused to do business with them and had come to Rent-a-Wreck.

"He wanted a certain size car, and the only one I had was behind three other cars, and I'd have to move them. And I don't know why," Dave says, "but I said, 'Okay, I'll let you have that one.' Well, as it turns out, *he's* a writer too, for *The New York Times.* On Monday he comes in and says, 'Could I write a story about you?' "

The article was featured on the front page of the second section of the *Times*. The resultant publicity was tremendous. Rent-a-Wreck made the first page of *The Wall Street Journal;* stories with titles like "Rent-a-Wreck—We Hardly Try" were syndicated in newspapers all over the country. Dave began a series of radio and television appearances that has not stopped; he has been on over four hundred radio shows, and on such national television shows as *Good Morning, America, The Tomorrow Show, Phil Donahue,* and *Merv Griffin.*

With all this publicity, Dave was soon haunted by people who wanted to buy Rent-a-Wreck franchises. Having been burned by his oversophisticated investing, he was not about to get in over his head. "Franchising is a whole different world," he told them, "and I was smart enough to know I can't do it." The would-be franchisors often stayed around to watch Dave in action on the lot. Others went home to start their own Rent-a-Wrecks without benefit of franchise. Realizing how much this could hurt his reputation, Dave "spent a small fortune applying for a federal trademark and registering it in all fifty states. I didn't want anyone to get us confused with some other operation with the same name that was running a poor business." Numerous used-car rentals began to open up under other names, as well. "Plenty of guys have copied us," Dave says, "and most of them went under."

Even though people were begging for franchises, Dave might never have gone into franchising if he had not met Geoffrey Nathanson. Geoff, a Los Angeles entrepreneur, had been a pioneer in cable television and pay television. Geoff had sold his cable interests for several millions and formed Universal Controls Corporation, a company specializing in remote-control television equipment.

The friend who introduced them thought there might be a way to combine Dave's success with Geoff's sophisticated business background. When the two men met to explore possibilities, the contrast between them was striking. Geoff was immaculate in tailor-made clothes, neatly trimmed dark hair, and a youthful air of corporate success. Dave was unshaven and dressed as always in blue jeans, T-shirt, and running shoes ("I'm the original runner, since way before it was a fad").

Rent-a-Wreck itself struck Geoffrey as being singularly unimpressive. "Who would want to rent a car here?" he wondered. Later he admitted to Dave that he really could not understand Rent-a-Wreck's success.

As for Dave, he jokes, "I usually try to keep people like Geoff out."

After that meeting, Geoff was not disposed to join Dave. Then a series of events conspired to convince him. First, as he drove home to Malibu that evening, he gave a lift to a man who was walking along the Coastal Highway with a gas can.

The passenger explained, "I have a Rent-a-Wreck, and it ran out of gas when the gauge read a quarter of a tank."

"Aren't you mad at them?" Geoff asked.

"Oh, no. He told me about it, it's my fault I forgot. I wouldn't say anything. It took me three weeks to get a car there—they're all booked up." He added, "Everybody knows about Rent-a-Wreck."

Geoff wrote the meeting off as a strange coincidence. Then the following week, his wife came home with a story. A friend of hers, an actress, was driving a 1966 Plymouth. When Geoff's wife asked if that was her car, she replied, "Oh, no, it's a Rent-a-Wreck. It's fantastic. It took me months to get this car, because they were all booked. This costs about the same as the new one they had, but it's much better. Besides, I had a light go out, and they were here in twenty minutes to fix it. You know about Rent-a-Wreck, don't you? Everybody knows about Rent-a-Wreck."

The following day the coincidences became too much to be ignored. Geoff's son told him he had met some people from England on the bus, who were on their way to Rent-a-Wreck. They had read about Dave Schwartz in the London newspapers.

"Something is pointing me to Rent-a-Wreck," Geoff concluded, and he set up a second meeting with Dave. This time the two men agreed to work together, despite the fact that Geoff's first suggestion was to change the name to Rent-a-Relic. "He's a very structured person," Dave remarks. "He wasn't sold on the name—like who wants to rent a wreck? He loves Rent-a-Relic. Well, I'm just not a Rent-a-Relic."

After several meetings, Dave and Geoff decided to collaborate on a manual titled, "A Turnkey Program into the Used Car Business," which they sold for $750. At this point they were convinced that franchising was too complicated. Surprisingly, most of the manuals sold to people in the new-car rental business who wanted to know the secret of Dave Schwartz's success.

"Then one day," Dave recounts, "a very successful businessman came down from San Francisco to see us. He brought along his attorney and his accountant; looked everything over, and bought the manual. Then he said, 'How about if I use your name?' So we worked out a deal for X dollars for the use of the name, Rent-a-Wreck. Then we did the same thing for another guy, and another one after that, and before you know it, we're not just selling a manual anymore, we're franchising. It just evolved."

The first Rent-a-Wreck franchise was sold on May 15, 1978, by Bundy American Corporation, a company formed by Dave and Geoff to act as franchisor. Each man invested twenty-five thousand dollars as start-up capital, and each owns an equal share of the business. Dave is chairman of the board, and Geoff is the company's president. "We're perfect together," Dave exclaims. "Neither one of us needs the money, so we just plow everything back into the business." Money is obviously not the primary motivating factor for either of the men, who are both wealthy. They are simply excited about creating something unique. As a result of their enthusiasm, Bundy American is now worth a fortune. Several large corporations have offered substantial cash payments plus a percentage of profits; Dave and Geoff have turned them down.

Bundy American Corporation's headquarters, atop the prestigious high-rise Kirkeby Center in West Los Angeles, offers quite a contrast to Dave's used-car rental lot a short drive away. The executive offices employ five secretaries and a franchising executive hired away from one of the top franchisors in the new-car rental industry. Dave himself has a spacious, well-furnished office that is larger than the entire building on his car lot and offers a spectacular view of Los Angeles. However, he still spends a full day at his Pico Avenue lot, and is in the vast office only two or three hours a week. Geoff, however, often spends eighty hours a week at Bundy American headquarters.

Dave devotes three days every other week to training Rent-a-

Wreck franchisees, who come from all over the country to learn from "the guru of used-car rental," as Dave has been called. "I'm like their car shrink," he says. "When they leave here, they know they can call me anytime from five in the morning on, and any evening. And they do." Teaching other people has sharpened Dave's own understanding of his business. "I've learned a great deal not only about the business," he says, "but about myself, too, just from expressing my thoughts and getting them on a conscious level."

Despite his casual appearance and personal style, Dave is anything but casual about training franchisees. He believes they must have complete control of the business the day they open. "It's like a restaurant that opens a month too early, and you go in there, and then you only remember how bad it was. Two years later someone tells you it's a great restaurant, but you remember that first week. I know of people who, to this day, won't use me because they remember the horrible car I gave them when I first started. You have to know this business from A to Z. If you know it from A to W, that's not enough, you'll find yourself in bankruptcy court. You gotta know A to Z."

Each franchisee receives the manual and will get a monthly company newsletter when he goes home. But Dave believes nothing printed can substitute for the in-person training he gives on his Rent-a-Wreck lot. It is not merely a classroom experience. During their three days there, the students observe the grand master in action. By the time they leave, they have become believers.

At a recent class, three new franchisees watched Dave handle the typical wary questions: "Do they run?" "Are they safe?" and so on. Dave had told them never to argue with a customer; when a cynical man called in, they got to observe this principle in action.

"How old are these cars?" the man asked. Dave confided later that he knew then and there that this caller was not interested under any circumstances.

"Oh, they're very old," he replied. "They're seventy-eights and seventy-nines."

"I mean, do they run?"

"Sir, they have eight to ten thousand miles on them. Some even have twelve thousand. You're taking a chance."

"Well, what do they look like?"

"Sir, a car that old is going to be all faded."

"I see. What are your rates?"

Dave flashed a grin at the students. "Two dollars a day and two cents a mile."

The man hesitated and then blurted out, "Nah, I can't take a chance."

"So," Dave comments, "he's one of the five percent that's turned off by the name Rent-a-Wreck. You've got to have a sense of humor about it. A guy like that won't even rent at two dollars a day."

"Finesse versus force" is one of the four principles Dave teaches all new franchisees. "I never, never argue with anyone. Did you ever see a cop get mad? Never. He might be jamming some guy in the ribs with his billy club, but he's smiling. The next time you get a traffic ticket, notice how polite the cop is. We're the same way. It's very low-key sell.

"I also preach quality cars and quality customers. You have to be selective about who you rent to. And I stress the importance of controlling—you've got to know what you're doing. That's what this training is all about." Dave believes, too, that it doesn't pay to knock the opposition. When a customer asks Dave what he thinks of a used-car rental agency down the street, he says, "I think they're great. I love them." End of discussion.

Summing up his franchisee training, Dave says slowly, "I don't just teach them how to make money—I teach them a business philosophy. I talk about greed. Sometimes we get into lengthy discussions on this subject. I explain how I used to be after the last buck when I was younger, and look where it got me then. When you're after the last buck, you don't get it, and when you're not after the last buck, somehow you just do. The bottom line is not numbers, it's peace of mind."

Franchisees are encouraged to hold out for quality customers by hard evidence that Dave's intuitive selectivity works: Rent-a-Wreck franchisees get liability insurance at rates that are reputed to be the lowest in the industry. "It pays off," Dave says. "It's those undesirables, those flakes we don't take, that get into accidents. So being selective not only keeps us from getting stiffed, it keeps our accident rate low."

Dave believes there's a right way and a wrong way to conduct any business, and his ambition is to teach franchisees the right way. Sometimes it isn't easy. Recently he accepted a franchisee "who had been running a place called Rent-a-Lemon for two years, and he was losing money. He didn't know what was wrong." It is against Dave's policy to switch a franchisee over, but the man was pleasant and his financial statement and reputation were both very good, so Bundy American accepted him.

"Well," says Dave, "it's like teaching an old golfer with all those bad habits how to do things right. It took me two weeks with this guy! I was a nervous wreck when he left. I thought I was going to have a breakdown. Everything I'd tell him, *everything*, he'd say, 'That's not the way I do it.'

"I'd say, 'I *know* you don't do it this way. You're losing money. *This* is how you do it.'

"He argued with everything. 'David, you only have one rate. I have six rates.'

" 'I know, but *this* is the way you do it if you want to make money.'

"It seemed like it took me forever to get through to him. But he finally turned around, and now he's making money—doing it our way."

While the new franchisees are in Los Angeles, they also spend some time with Geoff. "What a contrast!" Dave says, laughing. "Geoff's Mr. Clean and I'm Mr. Dirt. One time I had some important people coming in on Monday, and on Saturday over comes Geoff with his vacuum cleaner. Can you imagine? Here's this sophisticated businessman cleaning up my dirty office."

Actually, while Dave admits that his lot "would scare me to death if I walked in here as a customer," the office itself is perfectly organized. "There's not one thing out of order," he says proudly. "We know right where everything is. Our filing cabinets are perfect. Sure, it looks like something out of a Tennessee Williams play, but it's very workable."

A franchisee who visits Dave in his luxurious home in nearby

Beverly Hills will find an entirely different way of life. Dave and his lovely wife and two sons live in an Old English-style house, complete with wood plank floors, country kitchen, beamed ceilings, wet bar, and a wood-burning fireplace which occupies an entire wall of the living room. The living room faces a flowery back yard with a large swimming pool surrounded by deck chairs. The house and terraced yard also shelter the family pets and an occasional stray. Scooping up a ginger cat who has strolled into the living room, Dave says proudly, "Look at him —he looks just like Morris!"

Dave's love for cats is so strong it has even been known to influence a business deal. Bundy American had received twenty applications for franchises in New York City. Typically, Dave and Geoff took the time to be selective. One applicant, Joe Axelrod, was particularly impressive. Joe, a successful businessman, owns Olins Rent-a-Car Company, the largest independent car-rental company in New York State, with five locations in Manhattan. Dave finally went to see Joe at his offices on West Seventy-sixth Street. "Well, you know me," he says. "I'm dressed like I always dress. All these people in the office have on coats and ties. But what does he have in his personal office? *Two cats!* We hit it off immediately. Out of all those applicants, I picked Joe. We had good business reasons for selecting him, but also, he's into cats —just like me. I couldn't believe it!"

Most Rent-a-Wreck franchisees own car dealerships; many others have been involved with the major rental organizations, such as Hertz, Avis, National, and Budget. Bundy American recently negotiated a franchise for the entire country of Australia with a man who is the largest General Motors dealer in that country. Rent-a-Wreck's ability to be selective in franchisees obviously gives the company built-in quality control. Why would an experienced automobile dealer need a Rent-a-Wreck franchise? "Name and reputation," Dave says succinctly. "What's better— owning Ed's hamburger stand, or owning a McDonald's?"

Every new Rent-a-Wreck franchise opens to major publicity, organized by Mark Grody, head of the public-relations firm Bundy American employs. Dave is now on the road doing a grand opening every other week. The recent Rent-a-Wreck media event in New York City exemplifies how new franchises are received. "We were on five television stations for a total of eight times," Dave says gleefully, "and we were on radio nineteen times—that's in a single day! We opened with one hundred cars, and in four hours they were all rented out. Now New York's up to two hundred rental cars.

"You wouldn't *believe* the media party. We couldn't even believe it, everyone came. There must have been 125 media people there. I mean, we had *The New York Times*, the *Daily News, Newsweek, Time, Good Housekeeping, Air France*, even *Bride's Magazine*. Van Gordon Sauder, the president of CBS sports, was there. Gary Trudeau, the cartoonist. The media interest was just fantastic!"

Dave is not yet accustomed to this kind of publicity, despite the fact that it happens everywhere a Rent-a-Wreck opens. "Boy," he says, "they really get a kick out of billing me as the only chairman of a major corporation who goes around the country in jeans and running shoes. One newspaper said they can't even get me into corporate offices. That kind of stuff really turns me on. I think it's very funny. I mean, we're a business, but they treat us as if we're a *news* event. After all, how many companies make the evening news every time they come into a new market? That kind of publicity is worth millions.

"The week before the Ali-Holmes fight, a sportswriter from *The New York Times* called me up. Next thing you know, what's in the paper? Ten people picking the fights, people like Gary Trudeau, Steinbrenner, Woody Allen—and Dave Schwartz of Rent-a-Wreck. (And I was the only guy who picked it right!) My friends who saw it couldn't *believe* it. The nine best-known people in New York and me. Figure it out!"

8

BabyLand General™

What happens when you're twenty-one, poor, and have a crazy idea everyone laughs at?

"You don't give it up," says Xavier Roberts, chief-of-staff, founder of BabyLand General™ Hospital, and designer-physician to over a hundred thousand "Little People" in less than three years' time.

Who or what are Little People? In case you haven't heard, they are soft-sculptured babies, and anyone at BabyLand General Hospital will tell you, "They don't like to be called dolls." Furthermore, you can never *buy* Little People. They are only "up for adoption," complete with birth certificates, of course.

To some people, BabyLand General is strictly fantasy—or just plain childish. There is, indeed, a remarkable follow-through on fantasy—but there's nothing childish about it. Some 85 to 90 percent of the adopting parents are adults. The "adoption fees" may sound high at first, but many people consider these Little People an art investment. For others, the soft-sculptured babies are simply fun.

At BabyLand General Hospital, the original "adoption center," everything possible is done to carry out the fantasy and make the Little People irresistible. A staff of more than three hundred, including well-trained doctors and nurses dressed in white uniforms, is on hand to greet you. There's a maternity ward with bassinets and incubators, a fanciful Cabbage Patch delivery room, an expectant father's room, and an adoption office for eager parents. Following a delivery (or adoption-selection), new parents raise their hands and recite the Oath of Adoption. They are then presented with an official notarized birth certificate and adoption papers. One year later their Little Person™ baby will receive a birthday card to commemorate the happy occasion.

BabyLand General, "Home of the Little People," is located in Cleveland, Georgia, a sleepy mountain town of 1,600 about seventy-five miles northeast of Atlanta. BabyLand was founded by Xavier Roberts and five friends in September 1978. By 1981 it had become the area's largest employer and had been featured in *Time* magazine and on national television. Over a hundred thousand Little People had been adopted out. With adoption fees starting at $125 and going as high as $3,000, BabyLand General is a success in anybody's book.

Xavier Roberts, the creator of all this, has the devil-may-care look in his eyes to which any twenty-five-year-old, self-made millionaire is surely entitled. Not very long ago he was a good deal less affluent; his is truly an American rags-to-riches story. When Xavier was five years old, his father was killed in an automobile accident; the tragedy brought hard times to the widow and six children. When, in 1978, Xavier founded BabyLand, he had never known financial ease.

Today he seems unspoiled by his sudden, dramatic success. Typically, he wears jeans, a western-style shirt, cowboy boots, and a cowboy hat to work. At five-foot-seven, with a neatly trimmed dark beard and a pleasant air of self-confidence, he looks like a compact version of Burt Reynolds. An artist who has made a commercial success of soft sculpture, Xavier is also a businessman who knows exactly what he's doing.

The young entrepreneur explains, "When most people have a good idea and someone says, 'Oh, you can't do that'—they listen. That's their first mistake. I'd say with a good idea—and there are plenty of them—the keys to success are enthusiasm and follow-through. Don't give up, and don't listen to people who say you can't." Perseverance is not the only key to success, however, Xavier continues, "A good staff behind you is very important, and I've been lucky to have that. We've found other factors important in our success: uniqueness of product, creative display, high quality, and definitely, marketing." It's no wonder that Xavier is often asked what business school he attended.

Actually, the young entrepreneur was not a business major, but an art student at Truett McConnell College in Cleveland, Georgia, his home town. He got his start managing an arts-and-crafts shop in a nearby state park. Xavier never finished school. Because of money problems, he had to work full-time while in college. Initially, his artwork included "making just about anything—clay sculpture, jewelry, tapestries. Then I discovered soft sculpture."

Soft sculpture, an old German technique, had been used for years, but has only recently become popular in America. Most people had never been exposed to it when Xavier started. The medium fascinated him. Soft sculpture, he explains, is similar to sculpture in any medium, except that it is worked in fabric or other material with a soft texture. "I did some experimenting with it," he adds, "and developed my own style. I worked to create as realistic a soft-sculptured infant as possible." Soon Xavier began adopting out (selling) his babies at art shows along with his other work.

Smiling, Xavier will tell most people that he "found the Little People in a cabbage patch." Today the Little People come in both sexes, two colors, and two ages—infant and toddler. Each baby's skin, colored to have a lifelike appearance, is made of fabric that resembles a nylon stocking but will not snag or run. Babies come with many different hairstyles and hair colors. While the eyes are painted, every other feature—from the toes to the navel—is sewn. The standard newborn infant weighs from two to three pounds and wears real infant and toddler clothing.

"The most important thing," Xavier says in his deep Southern drawl, "is that each baby is an original work of art. We model them on real children, and we do everything to make them look realistic—from freckles or dimples to real baby clothes. That helps give them individual personalities, and that's what captures people's hearts. You see, no two of our Little People are just alike . . . except an occasional set of twins."

When the young artist began taking his Little People to art

119

shows throughout Georgia and neighboring states, the babies quickly demonstrated their appeal. Although he exhibited all forms of art, it was the soft-sculptured babies which attracted rave reviews. People found them cute, lovable, even pathetic-looking. The babies, Xavier explains, "just sort of took over because they were unique." While dozens of other artists competed in painting, for instance, Xavier's Little People were unique.

The very first babies sold for thirty dollars, a price which did not begin to compensate Xavier for his labor. Soon, however, he was able to raise his price to forty, then to fifty dollars, and so on. "People were calling me twenty-four hours a day," he says, "and it was simply a matter of the supply not being able to keep up with the demand. Raising my prices more didn't seem to make any difference. I still sold out of everything I was able to make. Before long I had developed a following, and people began to buy them as collector's items."

By February 1978, Xavier was devoting all his energies to making and marketing his babies. When he wasn't on the art-show circuit, he was at home in a small house trailer doing what he affectionately calls "making home deliveries." In April 1978 he decided to form a company to meet the demand for babies.

By then, Xavier had moved out of his trailer into a large frame house which he rented for $250 a month. "I couldn't afford the rent," he admits, "so I took in some other guys—but most of the house was used to start the company."

Since Xavier couldn't afford to pay anyone, his first three people—Linda Allen, Sharon Mauney, and Paula Osborne—each received 5 percent of the stock in exchange for a verbal promise of two years of their committed work and dedication. When Carol and Terry Blackwell joined the group, they each received 2½ percent of the stock. Xavier owns the remaining 80 percent of the company's stock. Xavier had met Linda at Truett Mc-Connell College; all the others were old high-school friends.

Linda Allen, now a vice-president whose duties have included public relations, explains, "At Xavier's suggestion, I came here soon after college. I was willing to work for only grocery money until the business got off the ground. I wanted to help develop a wonderful, fun idea." Sharon Mauney, who became secretary-treasurer, had put her new car up for collateral, believing that "my five-percent interest in the company would someday be very valuable."

Paula Osborne became "director of deliveries," or headed up production, among other duties. Carol Blackwell became purchasing agent, while Terry Blackwell took charge of building maintenance.

"It's so important to generate and maintain enthusiasm," says Xavier. Obviously, he does that well.

"I could never have done it alone," he continues. "It took other people to help follow through. And we kept each other enthused. We all believed in it."

A grin flashes over Xavier's face as he tells about the initial capital invested in the company. "The banks thought we were a bunch of crazy kids," he says, chuckling. "They couldn't see how we could ever do anything with this business on a large scale. All we were able to borrow was five thousand dollars—and in order to do that we had to put up two cars as collateral, mine and Sharon's. But after that we just kept putting the money back into the business every time we sold something, and then we'd make more babies.

"I got lots of good moral support from my mother, but being brought up poor, I knew that as far as money went I had to make it on my own. That was motivation, too.

"It was tough going," he confesses. "I had to use my credit card during those early days when I was short on cash. Finally I got behind on the payments and lost the card. Even today, I don't have a Visa card—but I don't go anywhere without my American Express!"

In 1978 the company was incorporated as Original Appalachian Artworks, Inc.; it does business under its trademark name, BabyLand General. The incorporated name reflects the fact that every product ever made by the company is original art, as well as the fact that BabyLand is located in the Appalachian Mountains, known for artistic creativity. When BabyLand started making the babies on a large scale, it operated partly as a cottage industry, since the business could not house a large work force. "The Appalachian folks around here are very good at making things with their hands," Xavier explains, "so we paid them based on what they could produce in an hour. I've lived here all my life, so I knew practically everyone, and I also knew what they were capable of doing."

Today most of BabyLand General's babies are born (not manufactured) in the Cabbage Patch, a special place in the mountains outside of Cleveland which is "top-secret," the hospital staff will tell you with a slight grin. There, nearly three hundred artisans lovingly hand-deliver babies under Xavier's supervision.

When the company was expanding and running out of room, the house Xavier rented was sold. Fortunately, his search for a new building led him to a vacant old medical clinic not far from the company's first location. (As Xavier comments, "In Cleveland, Georgia, nothing is very far from anything else.") The woman who leased the clinic to BabyLand supplied paint and materials, and Xavier and his friends provided the labor to clean and brighten the building. "She's terrific," Xavier says, beaming, "a really neat lady who's been very supportive. You wouldn't have believed this place. It had sat here vacant for almost twenty years.

"The strange thing about it was that everything had been left as it was. The doctors who had been here left filing cabinets, X rays, medical books—everything. You'd open a drawer and the stuff would be just lying there. It was as if somebody had left one day and never returned. I don't mean it was trash. There was no garbage—just tons of dust all over the place. So we had a real clean-up job to do. I bet we've painted and repainted the place at least a dozen times already."

Later, BabyLand also leased the first two floors of the large three-story house next door to the clinic, which had been the doctor's home. Today it serves as administrative headquarters.

Whether at BabyLand General Hospital or in an art- or gift-show booth, Xavier and his co-workers have always created an atmosphere which brought the babies to life. They are talked about as real children with real personalities who need homes.

When the company was first formed, the babies were sold only at art shows in Georgia and neighboring states on a direct-to-the-consumer basis. The first shops which asked to carry the line bought the babies at retail and made their own markups. "I was getting a few accounts at the art shows," Xavier states, "but I wasn't doing business on a wholesale basis. Finally we realized that we should be doing gift shows where we could sell to retailers. But it wasn't a matter of getting into them just like that. Not that art shows are easy to get into, either—we were competing with hundreds of exhibitors for space, and getting in only because we had a unique kind of art. But it doesn't work that way in the gift and trade shows.

"I'd have to say that getting into the wholesale shows was one of our most difficult problems. If you want to get a new product into the buyers' hands, you've got to work these shows. But it's not as easy as you'd think to even find them!"

Xavier leans back in his chair and laughs. "I didn't have a business background, so I had no idea how merchandise even got into stores. I mean, you never really think about how a product you buy in a shop ever got there. So we had to make call after call to find out where to go and who to talk to and how to get into the shows. There was no easy, set pattern explaining step by step, 'This is how you do it.'

"In the beginning, we knew there was an Atlanta merchandise mart, so we assumed there must be merchandise marts in other big cities like Dallas and Chicago, and that's how we sent letters out. Unfortunately, not every city calls its gift show a merchandise mart, so we had a lot of letters come back. But after we did one show, it led to something else, and slowly but surely we learned the ropes."

Most gift shows, Xavier points out, have a waiting list of at least two years. For the New York gift show, the biggest and best, the wait is five years. While BabyLand is still not in that one, the soft-sculptured babies are now shown in almost every other major gift show.

"Boy, I'll never forget that first Chicago gift show." Xavier grimaces. "We got hit by a real good blizzard. We made expenses, but that's only because we really hustled. Yeah, hustling is the name of the game. We could have gone up there and sat around and let the buyers go past. But we didn't. We'd grab them and just let them have it! That's really what it takes, because although we have a great product, it's expensive. So we'd pull them over to our booth and show them our babies.

" 'Do you mean to tell me this doll will sell for this price?' some people would ask.

" 'No, they don't *sell*,' we'd answer, smiling. 'This is the *adoption fee*.' Then we'd show them our birth certificates and adoption papers, and before you knew it the buyers would be hooked."

Although a few of the early shows were what Xavier bluntly calls "financial busts," he also adds that they were great learning experiences. And the young entrepreneur never got disheartened. "Whenever one of us would get discouraged," he explains, "the rest of us would pick that person up. There was never a time when we thought about giving up or that our business wouldn't succeed. We were never pessimistic. Even when we'd come back from a show without enough orders to pay our expenses, we'd say, 'Yeah, but so-and-so stopped by, and so did so-and-so, and I could tell they were very interested. I know they're going to give us an order!' "

One criticism Xavier heard often in the early days was "You're never going to get shop owners to fill out those adoption papers and other stuff. They just won't mess with it!" Today, however, almost two thousand shops across the country have become "adoption centers." As Xavier explains, "It was just a matter of educating them and getting them excited. The whole key is to generate enthusiasm about our marketing concepts, so it's very important that we work with the shop owner. I don't believe any product or idea can be marketed successfully unless it's taken from the drawing board with a great deal of enthusiasm. In our case, we've got to sell the shop owners on the entire concepts, from the birth certificates right on down to the special words we use—and don't use.

"For instance, we correct them in a nice way if they use the word 'doll' by saying, 'Oh, don't call him that, you'll hurt his feelings. He's a *baby*.' When they say 'buy,' we'll say 'adopt.' Before very long they're using those terms too. Then we'll talk about a certain bald baby having diaper rash, or mention how another curly-headed blond is fond of animals, and how another with freckles has been so naughty he has to be set in the corner. Before you know it, they start to talk about them the same way."

Display and positioning are also important in merchandising the babies. Whether it's a bald baby reaching up from a bassinet or a pigtailed girl with a cookie in a high chair, every baby is positioned to look like it wants to be picked up. BabyLand representatives explain to shop owners that "the babies will die if they're just left to sit on a shelf. It's up to the shop owner to put life in them." BabyLand insists that shop owners use the entire concept for marketing the babies. "If they don't, it won't work," Xavier explains, "and that's no good for anyone. Uniformity is just as important in our business as it is in a McDonald's franchise." One BabyLand requirement is that an adoption center begin with a minimum order of twenty-four babies, so potential parents can see that they're really one of a kind.

It's interesting to note that the more than two thousand BabyLand General accounts across the country are *not* toy shops. Adoption centers are located in stores frequented by adults—not children. Typically, they are exclusive gift shops and galleries. Many department stores, however, carry the babies, so children are likely to see them displayed in toy departments there. Since the babies wear regular children's clothing, some children's clothing stores use them as mannequins for attention-getting window displays.

The babies are more likely to be sold in galleries than toy shops because, as Xavier explains, "They are not toys. We discourage sales to children unless they're going to treat them with care and respect." Many of BabyLand's sales today come from repeat business. "If a family gets a girl," Xavier notes, "they'll most likely come back for a boy. The average family has two babies, and there's an amazing number of people who have three or four.

"You know," he adds, smiling, "when you look at the art some people buy—and what they pay for it—we're really offering a terrific value. Don't forget, this is a piece of art you can pick up, hug, and kiss. You can't do that with a painting. So many people are collecting the babies, too, and some want a Little Person from every edition. We know of a number of people with forty or fifty babies. One woman in Louisiana has seventy, and every one is accounted for in her will. The funny thing is that some people who purchased our first edition got laughed at, and now they're selling them at a big profit."

Babies from BabyLand General have come to be status symbols today. Some people believe this is true because they are recognized as expensive works of art. Others compare them to such items as designer jeans, which become status symbols because everyone recognizes their signatures—and high price tags. At present such "in" celebrities as Brooke Shields, Bette Midler, Diana Ross, Tammy Wynette, Marie Osmond, and Liberace have adopted babies from BabyLand General. And Amy Carter has a redheaded boy named Peanuts.

As collector's items, the babies from the early editions have increased considerably in value. Since every baby is unique and each birth certificate has its own code and matching baby registration number, a baby's "date of birth" can be easily authenticated. As a result, the owners of older babies have enjoyed much prosperity. One woman reportedly resold a first-edition standing baby recently for three thousand dollars—a very good return on a two-hundred-dollar investment after two and a half years!

To date, only two hundred Little People have been personally hand-stitched by Xavier; these special babies have a current value between five and ten thousand dollars.

BabyLand has had several different editions of Little People. Present adoption fees begin at $125 for unsigned Little People; signed, limited, or special editions such as Preemies, Christmas Babies, or Celebrity Babies, cost two hundred dollars and up. Each edition's accompanying birth certificates and adoption papers are easily identified by their own number, style, and color. Like most other forms of art, signed and limited editions are considered to be the most valuable. Xavier plans to stop "birthmarking" his signature on any of the babies, which is expected to make signed editions more valuable as time goes by.

In the fall of 1980, NBC's *Real People* inadvertently misquoted the $125 adoption fee at one thousand dollars. Instead of creating total havoc, the slip turned out to be a blessing in disguise when hundreds of people who had seen the show called to place orders for thousand-dollar babies. That figure, of course, made $125 and $200 babies look like real bargains!

Not one to miss an opportunity, Xavier quickly announced the Grand Edition—a thousand-dollar baby. These Little People come impeccably dressed in designer tuxedos and diamond cuff links. The young ladies wear evening gowns, diamond earbobs, and genuine mink coats. They come with a thousand dollars' worth of Little People play money, and their birth certificates and adoption papers are elaborately designed in gold and greenbacks green. As could be expected, BabyLand General Hospital delivered the Grand Edition, a special limited edition of a thousand babies, without missing a trick. Naturally, these babies "stand alone"—literally. They are toddler size instead of the regular infant size.

Simultaneously with the introduction of the Grand Edition came the arrival from the Cabbage Patch of the newest Little People, the Standing Edition. Designed by Xavier to express "the radiant appearance and personality of a toddler just learning to stand alone," they stand about toddler height—two feet or so—and adopt out for three hundred dollars each. Future plans include a Football Edition, with players and little cheerleaders to cheer them to victory.

BabyLand General has been invited to participate in the 1982 World's Fair in Knoxville, Tennessee; naturally, an International Edition will honor that occasion. Another recent theme is the Professional Collection—babies dressed as businessmen, surgeons, dentists, and so on. These Little People have added a new dimension to the company's marketing concept by appealing to professionals, and to their relatives and friends who buy the babies as gifts.

Adults frequently adopt Little People under the pretext that "They're really for the children." In fact, a parent is sometimes unaware that he or she is really the one who wants the baby. Xavier enjoys telling about one mother who came into an adoption center and fell in love with a baby. "Her child wanted a dollar-forty-nine toy"—he laughs—"but she kept saying, 'No, no, no, you don't want that. Don't you love this, honey?' Well, she kept insisting that her daughter should have a baby, and finally the two of them ended up with two different favorites. So the mother bought them both! Instead of buying the dollar-forty-nine toy she came in for, she ended up with $250 worth of babies."

BabyLand's market is apparently unlimited. People of all ages find the babies appealing. From nine months old to 102, from grandchildren to teenagers, from young singles to great-grandparents, everyone who loves children loves Little People. Even skeptical businessmen often succumb to the charms of the Little People; many have been seen cooing and cuddling the babies before leaving the adoption center. One woman wrote back a thank-you note saying that her Little Person satisfied her "minimal maternal instincts." It seems that Little People evoke the parental instinct in just about everyone. And, as one psychologist noted, for some people these babies symbolize the child, mate, or companion they would like to have.

But the staff at BabyLand General insists that babies won't sell by themselves, just sitting there on the shelves. Marketing requires a shot of "imagicillin," which starts the imagination flowing. BabyLand General takes credit for discovering this imaginary drug that gives each baby its own personality. Imagination brings a baby to life and makes it irresistible to any prospective parent with an ounce of compassion and love in his or her heart.

The babies come in an infinite variety. Some are bald, as are many newborns, and others have lots of yarn hair, sometimes short and curly, sometimes long and caught up in hefty ponytails. Each baby has its own facial expression, sometimes freckled or dimpled, sometimes, well, plainer. All babies have those special little details that mark them as works of art—tiny stitches which shape the small bumps of a turned-up nose, little ridges for toes and fingers, an "outie" belly button, and yes, even a softly rounded derriere fastidiously upholstered in a disposable diaper. Without question, all of the babies are eminently huggable.

As appealing as the babies are, it is undoubtedly BabyLand General's total marketing concept which has been responsible for the company's phenomenal growth. As Xavier explains, the concept came about naturally. "Right from the beginning, we ourselves put so much tender, loving care into our babies that we naturally felt adoption papers would be appropriate—the babies seemed so real. Once we did that, we started developing our own vocabulary, and every time one of us would use the wrong word, like 'sell' or 'customer,' the rest of us would correct that person. We'd all sit around at night and exchange ideas about how to add to the concept and what we could do to make the babies as real as possible, and this sort of thing really got contagious.

"One thing we do is let our imaginations work to give each baby an individual personality, and we teach our shop owners how to do the same. When a prospective parent (that's a customer, of course) is browsing around the store, an on-the-ball adoption agent (that's a sales clerk) might point out a particular baby, 'Oh, that's Otis Lee in the corner. He's been a very bad boy today.' Or she might say, 'Faith Caroline has a tummyache today. Here, if you pick her up and rest her head on your shoulder, I'm sure she'll feel much better.' Then the adoption agent might add, 'How about burping Faith Caroline while I check on Otis Lee?' " As Xavier points out, possibilities for generating interest in the babies are endless. A clerk might play patty-cake or change a diaper in front of a curious bystander. This kind of imaginative involvement creates interest in even the most blasé shopper. At BabyLand General Hospital it is obvious that imagicillin is commonly prescribed. The affectionate attitude toward the babies is not contrived, but ingrained in the enthusiastic staff. As Xavier notes, "It's just a matter of time before you automatically think and talk like this, and once you do, it's amazing how soon other people will react the same way. Sure, people will give you strange looks at first, but within ten minutes they catch on and they're doing the same thing and really enjoying it."

Although today the bulk of BabyLand's business comes through its more than two thusand adoption centers, nowhere is the fantasy so magnificently carried out as in the main hospital in Cleveland, Georgia. The rooms in the 1930s structure are cheerfully decorated to look like rooms in a real children's hospital. There's even a supply room where baby food and disposable diapers are stacked neatly on shelves. An expectant father's waiting room adjoins the adoption office, and Little People can be found happily playing in the recess room. There is also a feeding room with feedings daily at ten, two, and four.

As visitors enter the hospital, Little People greet them in the waiting room—some sitting at a table having a snack, others in strollers or cribs. Robin, an LPN (Little People Nurse) dressed in a crisp white nurse's uniform, greets guests and then conducts the grand tour. She is careful to put on her surgical gown and mask before she goes into the delivery room to check on the newly created line of Preemies, the tiny versions of Little People, born prematurely. Robin tiptoes past the sleeping babies and in a hushed voice reminds the visitors to do likewise. Before long, everyone is talking in whispers!

While there are wide-eyed children enjoying the tour, the adults almost always outnumber the youngsters. In the adoption room, a group of people can be seen with their right hands raised taking the Oath of Adoption. Staffers maintain that it's not terribly uncommon to see "new parents" with tears in their eyes. It is very common to see proud fathers grin as they accept cigars that say, "It's a boy" or "It's a girl."

Every member of the staff has stories to tell about the obvious emotion shown by some expectant parents. One pretty LPN says, "I remember once when three ladies came in, and one of them saw a baby she wanted. Well, they left for ten minutes so she could think it over, and she decided to come back. But when she got in here, a little girl was holding that particular baby and taking the Oath of Adoption. 'She has my baby!' the woman cried out, and she broke down and started crying right there. I didn't know what to do."

A young man dressed as a medic with a shiny tag reading: J. London, LPP (Little People Physician), explains, "It's amazing how some people come back days or weeks later and want a certain baby they remember. The baby's face just sticks in their mind until it becomes *their* baby."

"Some people come in full of doubts, but within minutes they get right into the swing of things here," explains another LPN. "Sometimes it's the look of a particular baby that appeals to them. Somebody might want a baby with curly red hair and freckles because 'he looks just like my husband.' Then the husband, who's been nonchalant up till then, gets interested and he starts to look for one with blue eyes and dimples like his wife. Before they know it, they walk out as the proud parents of two!"

"I get a kick out of the way some people hold their newly adopted babies," says a young intern. "The second that baby is in their arms, they act as if it were their own firstborn. You can just see the love in their eyes. Even some husbands who were the biggest doubting Thomases have acted that way."

Staff members agree that once a baby goes to its new home it can become a way for people to express their feelings. "Suppose a wife is mad at her husband," a BabyLand doctor explains. "She might say, 'Bruce Ashley thinks you're acting very grouchy today.' Another woman might say, 'Mary Jane just whispered in my ear that you should shut your big mouth ' I can just imagine some of the conversations that must go on. The reason I know is that I know what happens in my own case. When I have company for dinner, I might say, 'Michael Davy thinks it would be a good idea for you to stop smoking. It's starting to make it hard for him to breathe.' If the person still doesn't get the hint, I'll add, 'And besides, Michael Davy says you're making the whole place stink!' You see, I can get away with saying things I wouldn't say otherwise by speaking through the baby."

Like every other hospital, BabyLand General has an emergency room. Throughout the day babies can be seen leaving in the arms of their loved ones—often wrapped in bandages where a stitch or so has repaired a little rip. The emergency room is quite functional, and cares for hurt babies who are carried in, as well as those who come from all over the country via the U.S. mails and UPS. BabyLand General's doctor fees are "estimated on severity of injury or type of illness." For example, a broken ankle is $2.50, a new arm $6.00, a reconstructed belly button $2.00, a head transplant (without hair) $25.00, and a thorough bathing $10.00.

As one would expect, Christmas is the big season at BabyLand General. Elaborate parties are planned and publicized at adoption centers throughout the country, but the biggest of all is the one held at the hospital. Nurse Paula Osborne recalls, "Last Christmas there were people who stood in line five hours to have Xavier put his signature on their babies' bottoms!"

"We had more than ten thousand people during the Christmas

holidays," Xavier explains. "Most of them were people who had already adopted babies. They came to look at the hospital and join in the festivities. And they came to get their babies autographed. We had make-believe snow everywhere, and Santa and his elves came by. It was a big promotion, and we got a lot of good publicity out of it."

While the Christmas party was exciting, some people think it didn't compare to the Easter-egg hunt, a promotion that came about in a typically imaginative way. "Linda and I were talking," Xavier says, "and telling each other what we imagined a really great Easter-egg hunt would be like. Well, others joined in, and the more we talked, the more fun it sounded like, so we decided to make it come true and do it right here. We put up storybook characters all over the place and brought in sheep and baby chicks, and naturally a lot of bunnies—both real ones and costumed ones.

"We hid sixteen golden eggs, which awarded the finders with babies. Well, you never saw anything like it. We expected a few hundred people, but more than four thousand came. Half of them were adults who were stopping in after church, so they were dressed in their Sunday clothes. But that didn't stop them. They got down on their hands and knees and crawled around through the dirt and briars trying to find those golden eggs. If I would give some little kid a hint about where to find one, fifty adults would follow after him wherever he went! Hardly anyone left until the very last egg was found."

Not only is BabyLand General the largest employer in town, but it has put Cleveland, Georgia, on the map. Nearby Helen, an Alpine village which was once a logging camp, has long been a favorite tourist attraction in the beautiful Georgian foothills of the Appalachians. At first BabyLand was just a place people stopped while they were in the area, but it has now become an attraction in its own right. New York–Florida travelers often go hundreds of miles out of their way to see the famous hospital.

Currently there is no admission charge to the thousands of people who tour BabyLand General Hospital each year, since many adoptions result from tourist visits. The popularity of the hospital is one evidence of Xavier's total marketing concept.

"We're not going to be just a one-product company, by any means," he says. A man who thinks big, Xavier dreams of some-day building Another World—a sort of fantasyland where fantasy and reality meet. "Someday we plan to be another Disney. Don't forget, even Disneyland started out as only 108 acres and a good idea. Sure, we *started* small. In the early days we used to buy all our baby clothes at garage sales. We'd pick up little outfits for five and ten cents, and clean and mend them until they looked like new." BabyLand now has its own clothes-design team, and jobs out clothing which is designed in-house. The company is working toward the day when it will design and market children's clothes, and later adult designer clothes as well.

The drawing board for the future holds at least a hundred grand ideas. One is a line of life-size adult soft-sculptured dolls. "Just imagine all the new doors that will open!" Xavier says enthusiastically. "We've also had some television people express an interest in doing something with us. Then, too, recordings could tie in nicely. Children's books will be a natural—our own Linda Allen has been looking forward to writing and handling those. And we're looking into cartoons and greeting cards. Paula and the sales team are checking out jewelry—we already have BabyLand Stork necklaces available. Maybe we'll add other soft sculptures—and quilts. The possibilities are endless."

The company is presently self-sufficient and handles its own advertising, public relations, writing, photography, sales, com-puter work, and accounting. Xavier adds, "One of the problems we've had has been growing pains. We've grown so fast these past couple of years that we've had to be careful not to get in over our heads. Also, because we're all good friends we get some of the problems of a close-knit family business. Recently we've brought in some outside professional management to take some of the load off us, and as we continue to expand we'll have to do more of this. We've also developed some of our own people into top-notch management."

Picking up a pencil, he pauses reflectively for a moment. "Sure, I think of myself as an artist," he says, "but I'm realistic and I recognize the business end of what I'm doing. I don't believe any artist can be successful unless he's also business-oriented. Of course, there are times when I'd rather be working with some artistic endeavor than running a business, but I feel very fortunate in having so many outlets for my creativity in this company—when there's time! There's never a dull moment around here."

Xavier has come a long way in the three short years since he began his company in a small house trailer. The young artist who once had to put his car up as collateral now owns two Mercedes, an MG, and a vintage silver Jaguar. His new home is an ongoing conversation piece in Cleveland. An architectural dream, the house is a meticulously crafted conglomerate of lovely arches, odd angles, pools and splashing fountains, skylights, bay windows, mirrored walls, elegant chandeliers, track lights, and everywhere, masses of green plants in pots and hanging baskets. Separate guest quarters are joined to the main house by a wooden bridge. Another bridge, over the huge heated covered swimming pool, connects the second-story bedrooms to an observatory and a row of ceramic, photographic, and design studios above a large greenhouse. There are also two Jacuzzis and a two-story waterfall.

For Xavier, his home serves as a refuge where he can contemplate the exciting future of Babyland General. "And being young and idealistic," he says, "it's hard to know which channels you really want to go to—but the opportunities for this company are unlimited! This will be a billion-dollar-plus business someday. That amount may sound enormous now, but just wait and see what we do."

He grins and adds, "After all, if you ever want to be big, first you've got to think big."

9

The Toughman Contest ™

"HOW TOUGH ARE YOU?" reads the headline of a poster in a neighborhood tavern in Cleveland's near west side. A large fist beside the headline points a challenging finger: "We're looking for the toughest man in Cleveland. Could it be you?"

The poster solicits anyone eighteen or older who weighs between 175 and 400 pounds. "Barbouncers, professional athletes, bar brawlers, construction workers, college students, firemen, farmers, etc., etc." Anyone with professional boxing experience and anyone who has won five or more sanctioned amateur fights in the past five years is inelegible. And, the poster warns, there will be "No biting or kicking."

A total of thirty-two men will be selected to compete in this Toughman Contest. The winner the second evening will receive a thousand dollars and the runner-up five hundred. But everyone who wins his bout the first night will receive a trophy—*after* he returns to fight the second night as well.

As many as one hundred such Toughman Contests will take place this year throughout the United States and Canada, all brought to you by Ardore Ltd. Ardore is owned and operated by Arthur P. Dore, an imaginative entrepreneur from Bay City, Michigan. Art and his longtime friend Dean Oswald, a vice-president of Ardore who has an interest in the company, originated the Toughman Contest in 1979. Both men had been amateur fighters and had gone on to train, manage, and promote their own fighters. Dean had also boxed professionally, and is currently a United States boxing coach.

The first Toughman Contest was just for fun. "We had seen some amateur boxers," Art recalls, "who were great big guys but just couldn't fight a lick! We'd stop off at a bar after a fight like that, and all the young guys would gather around and tell us, 'Man, those guys couldn't fight! They stink! Why, Joe over here, he could lick every one of them.'

"Dean and I heard this so often that one night we finally said, 'Okay, you guys think you're so damn tough? We'll put all you guys together in a fight, and we'll *see* who the toughest man is. We'll just match you up, two at a time, until there's only one man left. He'll be crowned the toughest man in Bay City!' "

Art, a big man himself at six feet and two hundred pounds, leans back and grins. "That's how it started. We just thought it up one night at a bar, and decided to have some fun. We never gave a thought to making money at it."

In May 1979, Ardore put posters up around Bay City offering a total of one thousand dollars in prizes. Twenty-eight men signed up for the first Toughman Contest. "Now, that's not bad for a town of about fifty thousand," Art comments. "There was no promotion, no advertising, although the local newspapers did pick it up. But once those guys signed up, it really caught fire. In a town the size of Bay City, with twenty-eight tough guys talking it up in the bars, the word gets around like crazy. Tickets were ten bucks a head, and the place holds thirty-five hundred. Well, we had to turn people away at the door!"

The same thing happened at the second contest. Figuring they might be on to something, Art and Dean promoted this one in Marquette, Michigan, a town of about fifteen thousand. "Marquette's in the upper peninsula," Art explains, "out in the back woods, and we figured we'd draw some of those tough lumberjack types. And boy, did we!" About five thousand people flooded to the contest from all over the upper peninsula; once again, the Toughman Contest drew a standing-room-only crowd.

"We held one more fight, in Flint, Michigan, to see if this thing was for real," Art continues. "When the same thing happened, we were positive we were onto something that had the potential to be really big. And we knew that if it was going to work, we had to have a game plan, because once it caught on, we'd have every Tom, Dick, and Harry doing it too. That's the American way."

Art believed it was vital to establish a national reputation for the Toughman Contest in the shortest possible time. To do that, the company went all-out and promoted the First Annual U.S. and Canadian Championship Toughman Contest, scheduled for September 20 and 21 in 1979. In order to draw contestants from both countries, Ardore sent out over forty thousand full-size "How Tough Are You?" posters to bars and factories. The prizes were meant to be alluring, too: $50,000 to the first place winner, $20,000 to the runner-up, and $5,000 each to the men in third and fourth place. Applicants were considered in light of the rules Ardore had formulated by now—no professional experience, less than five amateur wins in the past five years. Ninety-five fighters were accepted.

Of those, sixty-four showed up for the contest, which was exactly the number Art was shooting for. All sixty-four men passed the physical exam, and on the first night of the tournament, all sixty-four men fought in single elimination rounds. The second night, Saturday, the thirty-two winners were paired up; then the sixteen winners of those matches were paired up again, leaving eight winners. Then there were four, and finally two men fighting for the championship. "The champion Toughman had to beat four guys in a single night to win that title," Art says. "Man, you've *got* to be tough to do that!"

Art has always been a man who thought *BIG*, and it took that kind of thinking to launch the Toughman Contests in a big way. The First Annual U.S. and Canadian Championship didn't take place in a small arena in some out-of-the-way town, but in Detroit's Silverdome. Of course, like every creative entrepreneur, Art heard his share of negative predictions. "Nobody believed it," he says, laughing. "Nobody believed I was going to go out and pick out a bunch of guys off the street and let them fight, and then give fifty thousand dollars to the winner! They thought it would never happen—but it did. We drew around fourteen thousand people. Yes, we took a little gas, but we were expecting to. We looked on it as an investment, and it was a good one. We established ourselves, we gained the credibility we needed, and we got fantastic publicity. After that, we were on our way!''

Ardore made another important investment about this time— in legal fees. Art, an experienced businessman, knew it was vital to protect the Toughman concept by getting trademarks, copyrights, and service marks on everything. "We got the whole intellectual property, so to speak," he says. "It's our idea, and we weren't about to let someone come along and steal it."

Since then, there have been a number of attempts to infringe on copyright. One Ohio man, for instance, tried to promote what he called a Roughman Contest. "Now, you can't do that!" Art says indignantly. "Obviously, people are going to think it's a Toughman Contest. We had to get an injunction ordering him to cease and desist." Art does not hesitate to protect his property in this fashion. "We're running a first-class show," he explains, "and we're establishing our reputation. This is our profession, and we don't want anyone coming in and getting a free ride. Anyone who thinks he's going to do that had better be ready to spend a lot of time in court, because I'm going to have him there. We don't have any other choice!"

Ardore has been very careful to protect its copyrights and trademarks in every way possible. Recently, for instance, ESPN, "The Total Sports Network," featured a Toughman Contest on national cable television. Throughout the evening, the broadcaster periodically told the viewing audience, "If any of you out there are thinking about having your own Toughman Contest, please be advised that you will be infringing upon copyright and trademark rights owned by Ardore Ltd." Already a multimillion-dollar business, the Toughman Contest is obviously well worth protecting.

Two years after the original "just for kicks" tournament, the Toughman Contest is nationwide and thriving. It has been featured in national media, including *PM Magazine* and *Real People;* and Art has appeared as a one-hour guest on the *Phil Donahue Show* (where he made a big hit with the women). The healthy growth of the contest seems to follow the pattern set by other Art Dore business ventures. A self-made man, Art started his own demolition business "tearing down homes and selling the lumber" with nothing but a crowbar and a sledgehammer. Dore and Associates Contracting Company is now one of the world's largest demolition and contracting firms, and has demolished more than fifteen thousand buildings, including many high-rise office buildings all over the world. Part of the company's success is owed to such Dore innovations as new explosive techniques and large trailers to carry debris.

(Incidentally, the fact that nowadays Art travels all over North America promoting the Toughman Contests and overseeing his demolition business has led to an "in" joke. When friends call and hear he's out of town, they'll ask, "What's he having knocked down today—buildings or bodies?")

In addition to extensive real-estate holdings, Art owns seven other businesses, including a country club and Aerospace America, a missile manufacturer. He also sponsors the Art Dore Boxing and Athletic Association, a nonprofit corporation set up to give inner-city children "a place to go to get off the street." Ardore Ltd. also owns professional prizefighters, two of whom Art claims will be contenders for the world championship in the near future.

Despite his financial interest in pro boxing, Art believes that the Toughman Contest is destined to become the biggest thing in boxing. Already the contests are drawing crowds unheard-of in boxing circles, for anything short of professional title fights. One reason for this is undoubtedly the professionalism of the Toughman promotion. Traditionally, boxing has depended almost entirely on sportswriters. Ardore, however, is not just after sports fans, but after anyone who likes to be entertained, and has taken full advantage of the drawing potential of television advertising.

Toughman Contests are promoted in action-filled thirty-second commercials. "We show them guys getting knocked out, boom, boom, boom," Art says. "We advertise that the maximum weight is four hundred pounds—people want to see the big guys fight. Now, there's probably not going to be anybody weighing four hundred pounds, but just saying that puts an image in people's mind of this giant in the ring. And we tell them, 'No biting or kicking.' Well, of course there's no biting or kicking, you never could do that. But it gives people the impression of a real brawl. When they hear that, they figure, 'Anything else goes.'

"What it all boils down to," he says, "is putting bodies in the seats. That's the name of the game."

"Putting bodies in the seats" has been increasingly difficult in professional boxing. With the exception of championship and top contenders' bouts, it is widely considered almost impossible to draw sizable crowds. Art believes the reason for that is the public's attitude toward pro fights. "There's a lot of fans," he says, "who think that the pro fights are fixed. That really turns a lot of them off. But with the Toughman fights, they *know* no one's going to take a dive. Everyone's coming to fight."

One of the excitements of a Toughman Contest is that it is anybody's guess who will win. Art explains that this is another reason for the large gates. "If I have a professional boxer, naturally I'm very careful about who I let him fight. If I thought somebody was going to beat him up, I wouldn't put my boy in the ring with that fellow. There's no way I'm going to let my fighter get beat up. You build your fighter's record by getting him fights you know he can win. And the boxing fans know, too, so there's no way to attract them to these professional fights."

Another big appeal of Toughman Contests is the fact that thirty-six men from the local community participate. This means that a high percentage of people in the crowd know at least one of the fighters. In smaller cities, people are likely to know several contestants. And each contestant has his own following. "If they know the guy," Art explains with a grin, "half of them are cheering him on and the other half want to see him get the hell beat out of him. But as far as *I'm* concerned, I never care who wins. It doesn't matter one iota to me, and believe me, that's important. That way the man-in-the-street knows this is for real."

Although every Toughman Contest has plenty of action, the boxing is strictly supervised according to the Queensbeery Rules of Boxing. "Sure, we get some static from the boxing commissions in certain states," Art admits. "But that's because of the way we promote the fights. They don't like to hear us talk about all the blood and guts, and they don't like it when our posters mention barroom brawlers. They think they're purists. *But* they don't put anybody in the seats."

Some boxing commissions have frowned on the fact that in a typical Toughman Contest the sixteen fighters remaining on the second night fight a round robin until a winner is declared. Art explains that this is not as hard on a man as the critics imply. "Don't forget, our contestants are only fighting three ninety-second rounds per fight. So the man who wins will fight a maximum of twelve two-minute rounds if all his fights go the distance—which rarely happens. Now, that's equivalent to a six-round professional fight, *and* the fighter has long rest periods between bouts, while a pro only has sixty seconds between rounds.

"Then, too, the two guys who go that far wouldn't make it if they weren't in darn good condition. The guys in the best condition are the ones who make it to the end. The losers really don't last that long in the ring. It's a matter of the survival of the fittest, and the guys who fight to the end of the second night are usually the fittest."

Art is dead set against any Toughman contestant getting seriously injured in the ring. "We're very careful to make sure nobody gets hurt badly," he emphasizes. The secret to protecting contestants, he explains, is to have good people at ringside. The Toughman Contests use professional referees, and Ardore is very selective about who handles the microphone. Art explains, "The guy on the mike controls the fight. And believe me, he's going to stop it the minute he sees somebody getting badly beat up."

As the Toughman Contest is presently designed, Ardore has to deal with the boxing commission in each state it promotes a contest in. Since a few commissions have rejected the Toughman Contest, Art has occasionally been advised to make changes in the contest so that it would no longer fall under the jurisdiction of any boxing commission.

"We won't do that," he replies. "We're in the boxing business and we believe that what we're doing is *good* for boxing. We expect to be sanctioned someday by the boxing commission in every state. I know there are some promoters who put on contests where guys in street clothes get in the ring and anything goes. They use karate, boxing, wrestling. They kick and scratch —they mutilate each other. Those promoters don't care what happens to the contestants. In fact, there was one fight like that down in Florida where a guy got kicked in the groin, and later a surgeon had to remove one of his testicles. Another guy got seriously injured by being kicked in the head while he was down on the floor. Now, that is ridiculous. We don't want any part of things like that."

Part of the success of the Toughman Contests is due to the professional supervision of the fights. Art himself goes to every Toughman Contest held in a city which has never had a contest before. "I just want to make sure nothing goes wrong," he says. He points out that if the bouts were not controlled, it would become increasingly difficult to attract contestants. "It's important for us to build a good reputation among the contestants," he says. "We can't afford to have somebody get hurt. If we let them get in the ring and kill each other, we'd only attract the crazy men the next time we came to town. But when we finish a contest, they can't wait for us to come back. They want to know when the next one will be. They want to start training, and if they know we're coming back, they'll train for a year so they can do better the next time. What's more, that's all they talk about for a year.

"This year we'll be doing our second show in Davenport, Iowa. Last year we sold out, and this year it's another sellout. We've already got our fighters lined up—a whole bunch of them have been training for this year's contest. And the whole town is talking about it—sportscasters, newspapers, they're all waiting for us. Doing it the second time is a piece of cake!"

Nobody in boxing expected Ardore to establish such a successful track record. Most experts thought that matching up amateurs off the street had to be a losing proposition. Furthermore, getting the contests off the ground was bound to be expensive. Art confirms that it takes a lot of money up front to reserve an arena for two nights, and more to advertise and promote a contest. "This is definitely not a business for someone who doesn't like to take risks," he says, chuckling.

The Toughman Contest was also rejected by the media at first. Art points out that most sportswriters initially refused him when he approached them about coverage for his fights.

"This ain't no sport," they'd say, "it's a circus."

"Have you ever seen one?" Art would reply.

"Well, no."

"Come and see it," and he'd offer them tickets.

"You ought to hear them now," he says. "They'll say, 'You know, when you first started this, I was kind of skeptical. Now I'm getting to like it. It's really exciting.' "

Art scratches his neatly trimmed beard. "Those are the same sportswriters who used to tell me it wasn't a sport. Sometimes they'd say they didn't want to cover it, and I'd say, 'Okay, thanks anyway, fellas.'

" 'Hey, wait a minute,' they'd say. 'Can you get me six tickets?'

" 'But if it's no good, what do you want tickets for?'

"Right away they were telling me something—*people wanted to see it.* Even the sportswriters who didn't want to cover it wanted to see it. *It had appeal.* Of course, once those reporters had actually seen a Toughman Contest, they became our biggest boosters. When we go back to a town the second time, we have their full support."

Sportswriters were not the only ones who were skeptical in the beginning. In some cities Art approached local entertainment promoters and asked them to handle advance publicity for a contest in return for a percentage of the profits; often he was turned down. However, he enjoys telling how one promoter became a believer. Gary Cheses, the owner of Entertainment Services in Columbus, Ohio, is a prominent promoter with a national reputation, and Art was sure he would be effective with the Toughman organization. "But I could tell I wasn't getting through to him," Art says. "Gary listened carefully to what I had to say, but I knew he had to be thinking, 'Hey, who is this guy, anyway?'

"Finally I gave him some complimentary tickets and said I hoped he'd come to the contest.

"He did. When I saw him, I went over to ask what he thought.

He looked at the sellout crowd and said, 'Something is sure working right.'

"I could tell by the look in his eye that he had become a believer." Today, Gary handles the advance work for many Toughman Contests, including advertising, ticket sales, and promotion.

Dean Oswald has also been invaluable in setting up and promoting contests. Because of his longtime experience as a fighter and manager, Dean knows just about everybody in the country in boxing circles. Whenever Ardore needs a contact in a new city for locating an arena or any other detail related to boxing, Dean knows whom to call.

Art envisions eventually having a franchise network where individuals in different parts of the country will be responsible for setting up Toughman Contests in their areas. He expects it to take some time before this is possible, however, because "We need experienced people. This thing is quite controversial in some areas, and we can't afford to make any mistakes."

From an impulsive idea, Ardore has created a big enterprise in the Toughman Contests, and running the business takes know-how. One of Ardore's key people, Joe Goldring, has extensive public-relations and advertising experience in the retail field. As director of operations, Joe has played a major role in coordinating efforts within the organization, so that it is now possible to have several contests going on simultaneously in different parts of the country. "This is a business that has to be done on a large scale to be profitable," Joe says. "It's like the automotive business. If a manufacturer only made a handful of cars, each car would have to cost a million dollars, and the manufacturer would still go broke. But if they make a million cars, they can make a fortune. The same thing is true in this business. You can't make any money on three or four shows a year. But it will work if you put on forty or fifty."

Joe believes every town of over twenty-five thousand people can support a Toughman Contest. "The most important thing is arena availability," he explains. "Take Lima, Ohio. That's a town of about seventy thousand, and we had a sellout crowd there of three thousand. But if Lima had an arena that held ten thousand, we'd fill it up."

Art foresees a time when North America will support as many as five hundred Toughman Contests every year, with local tournaments leading to state tournaments and then to regional contests, and regional winners fighting in the U.S. and Canadian Championship. The annual championship is already restricted to winners. "After our first championship tournament," Art explains, "we stopped taking just anybody off the streets. Now it's a tournament only for the winners from all over. We expect to have eighty local contests this year, so we'll have a lot of tough guys show up at the championship."

The 1979 championship winner was Roosevelt McKinley, a construction worker from Ann Arbor, Michigan, who checked in at six-foot-two and 215 pounds. Roosevelt, a sanctioned amateur boxer from 1973 to 1976, had participated in the 1976 Regional Olympic Trials. Having then retired from boxing, he founded the Ann Arbor Boxing Club. "I wanted to help the kids —they need somebody like me to keep them off the street," Roosevelt says. When he decided to try for the championship, Roosevelt put himself in training, running four to five miles every night and sparring fifteen rounds a day for six weeks. His dedication paid off to the tune of fifty thousand dollars—a classic storybook ending. Roosevelt used half his winnings to open a new youth facility in Ypsilanti, Michigan, a suburb of Ann Arbor. "I had some offers to turn pro after winning my title," he explains, "but I feel I belong with the kids. Some of my kids don't have anything worthwhile in their lives except for the club."

Mike White, who at seven feet and three hundred pounds is appropriately called The Giant, won the 1980 championship. Mike met Art at a Toughman Contest in Columbus, Ohio, where Mike was employed in a tall man's clothing store. "I saw this great big guy up there," Art recalls, "and he was strong but he couldn't fight a lick! He got beat, but he came to me afterwards and said, 'Boy, that was a lot of fun! I'd like to try that again.' It turned out he was thinking of moving to Saginaw, Michigan, and I told him we could put him in one of the tournaments there if he did."

Mike did move, and trained hard for his next fight. In his second contest, in Flint, Michigan, he knocked out five men in a row. From there he went to the championship and won the fifty-thousand-dollar prize. Mike has now turned pro and become one of Ardore's fighters. Although Mike has a lot of work to do, Art thinks the big fighter has a good chance as a pro.

American Cinema Productions has capitalized on the drama of the Toughman championships with the movie *Tough Enough,* released in October 1981 and starring Dennis Quaid, Warren Oates, Pam Grier, and Stan Shaw. The movie tells the story of a young boxer who wins $100,000 in the World's Champion Toughman Contest. Actor Warren Oates plays a convincing Art Dore—full beard and all. Fights and crowd scenes in the movie were filmed on the spot at real contests.

Toughman Contests attract men from every walk of life. Contestants have included attorneys, doctors, preachers, and numerous politicians. And it's a rare contest that doesn't attract at least one policeman, and often several. Even the most unusual occupations turn up; one contestant in Louisville, Kentucky, was a male go-go dancer.

Whoever is manning the mike at a Toughman Contest gives each contestant a nickname if he doesn't already have one. One contestant told Art to call him Preacher, since he actually was one. "You've heard about turning the other cheek," Art says with a laugh. "Well, that's what this guy did. He got slugged on one side of his face, and he literally turned around and got it on the other side! The fans just went wild."

In any contest, the crowd quickly picks its favorites. Art explains that the first night of a contest, "It's a comedy, because there are a lot of guys who don't know much about boxing." The second night, winners fight winners, but a new element of risk is added. While on the first night fighters are matched according to size (usually within ten pounds of each other), the second night is "the luck of the draw."

"So a 175 pound man could end up matched with a 280 pounder," Art explains. "That's one reason we wait until the second night to give them their trophies. All the first-night winners get a good-looking trophy, and they really take pride in them. Some of them might not show up for the second night if it wasn't for that trophy. They might be afraid of who they'll be matched with, and maybe they're a little stiff—they found out boxing isn't as easy as they thought."

On the second night of a contest, the boxing is much more skillful, and the fans are more excited. If the house was not sold out the first night, it will be the second, because last night's fans have returned with their friends to root their favorites on. After a fighter has won his second fight of the evening, the tempo picks up, with the theme from *Rocky* playing after each victory. Knowing that it's getting tougher and tougher to win, the crowd gets wilder, until everyone is jumping up and down. Nobody leaves the stands until the champion is determined. "When the final bout is fought," Art says, "you've never seen so much excitement in your life!"

The vast majority of Toughman contestants exhibit good sportsmanship. "Almost without fail," Art says, "no matter how mad they are at each other in the ring, they'll shake hands or embrace after the fight. You know, these are guys who live in the same community, but they probably never met before they climbed in that ring. I get the feeling some of them will be best buddies for the rest of their lives. That guy might have whipped you, but boy, nobody better say anything bad about him, or they're gonna be in trouble!"

With a slight smile, Art admits that there is an occasional exception to the rule of good sportsmanship. "We had an incident in Des Moines where a guy got knocked out, and he was sore because he thought the referee had given him a fast count. He wouldn't shake the winner's hand, and when the two of them stepped out of the ring, he actually took a swing at the winner! And he got knocked out *again!* Needless to say, that caused a lot of excitement. The audience loved seeing him get what he had coming."

Anything can happen at a Toughman Contest, and happen fast. Art recalls another amusing incident in Wheeling, West Virginia. "We had just finished the first fight when a man and a little kid got into the ring. It happened so fast that the police at ringside just stood and watched. Well, the man got down on his hands and knees and started to let the kid punch him. And *then* a drunk climbed into the ring and started going after the man. So the two of them are up there swinging it out bare-fisted, and I'm yelling to the cops, 'Get them out of there!' In the meantime, the crowd was loving it. They thought it was part of the show!''

Art enjoys announcing contests and, as many as he's done, still doesn't know what to expect from the Toughman crowds. "Once in Cleveland," he says, "I was chatting on the mike to kill some time while a fighter's hands were being rewrapped. It was taking too long, and the crowd got restless and started to boo. So I said, 'You guys out there who are making all the noise, you think you're so tough! Well, let's see you get in the ring here, and see what you can do. There's room for one more.' And the next thing you know, dozens of guys started coming out of the stands —they wanted to get in the ring! I had to announce, 'Say, fellows, I was only kidding. We don't have any more room for tonight.' ''

So far Ardore has never had trouble attracting fighters. Art feels this is because the Toughman Contest offers the typical contestant an opportunity he can't get anywhere else. "Here's a guy, he's in his early twenties and he's never fought. But he's been watching television and thinking, 'I know I could do that. I beat the hell out of Joe down at the bar.'

"Now, if he wants to fight," Art continues, "where can he go? He can go into the Golden Gloves, or AAU boxing as an amateur. But if he does that in his early twenties, he'll have to fight open class, even though he's never had a fight in his life. This means he'll be fighting experienced fighters—some of them guys who have had 100, 150 fights. He's going to get the hell beat out of him! Some seventeen-year-old kid is going to make him look like a fool. So the guy has no place to go. The Toughman Contest is his chance."

Young, inexperienced men are not the only Toughman contestants. "I've talked to a lot of guys," Art says, "who used to fight, say ten years ago. They want to go for one last hurrah and prove themselves all over again. It's a very macho thing."

With obvious pride, Art points out that in the first year of the contests, seventeen fighters went on to turn pro. "I'll tell you something," he adds. "There's one thing these guys got that many professional fighters don't, and that's heart. The ones who make it to the top in our contests aren't quitters. They've got guts, and that's what it takes to be a top fighter.

"Do you know what's going to happen within the next couple of years or so? You're going to see a heavyweight contender for the world championship being interviewed on television, and they're going to ask him, 'What's your background as a fighter?'

"He's going to reply, 'Man, I came from off the street and I got in a Toughman Contest and I won it. From that I turned pro, and here I am!'

"That's bound to happen sooner or later, and when it does, just imagine the credibility we're going to have."

Art's innovative ideas extend beyond the Toughman Contest to professional boxing. "We're going to promote a professional prizefight," he explains enthusiastically. "I mean, a real prizefight, where the winner gets all the money and the loser gets nothing —a winner-take-all fight. If you do things that way, people will *know* those guys are there to fight! You take the last Duran/Leonard fight, where they each got something like five million dollars just for showing up. What do they care who wins? They both get their money. My idea is to give all the prize money to the winner. In the old days that's how they did it, and I think they had the right idea. I don't think Duran would have quit so quickly because of a bellyache under those conditions."

Art and his wife, Shirley, have six sons and two daughters. All three of the sons who are old enough to qualify are amateur fighters. When asked whether he would allow one of his own sons to be in a Toughman Contest, Art quickly says, "Yes. Now, as far as professional boxing is concerned, I would never encourage my son or anyone else to stay in it unless he looked like he would someday be a top contender. Otherwise, you just take a lot of abuse and get nothing in return."

Women are not found in the ring at a Toughman Contest, although Ardore did once hold a Toughwoman Contest. The contest made money, "but it was just a novelty," Art says, "a one-time, one-shot type of deal. We don't plan to do it again." A Toughman audience, however, is usually about 30 percent female. "And they love it!" Art exclaims. "They're the most vocal fans." One reason the contests draw women is that they are held on Friday and Saturday nights, while professional boxing has traditionally been a week-night event. Art feels that many women object to their husbands going out on week nights to see a boxing match. And if pro boxing did take place on the weekend, women wouldn't want to go, and they certainly wouldn't want their husbands to go without them. "It's different with a Toughman Contest," Art explains. "The men can bring their wives. What we have here is entertainment for the entire family. It's just a fun time for everyone!"

One sign that the Toughman Contest is here to stay is its loyal group of fans. Ardore now prints schedules of coming events to mail to fans who call long-distance asking where the nearest tournament is. "These people go from town to town and make a weekend out of it," Art says with a chuckle. "And they have a helluva time."

In fact, with its growing core of die-hard fans, the Toughman Contest has achieved a real sign of success in today's entertainment world: its very own set of groupies!

10

Celestial Seasonings®

"I didn't pick herbs as a child," says the bright-eyed young executive, "but I did know every rhubarb patch, raspberry patch, apple tree and apricot tree, every kind of gooseberry and chokecherry in the valley." He sips a cup of Red Zinger, an herb tea which is, as the package says, "a real taste of the blendmaster's art!"

Since then, the blendmaster himself, Mo Siegel, *has* picked the rose hips and peppermint leaves which are among the ingredients of Red Zinger. Today, at age thirty-one, he no longer does. Instead, he sits at ease—often in blue jeans—in the office of founder and president of Celestial Seasonings, a seventeen-million-dollar company. He wants it to be a hundred-million-dollar company by 1988, and those who know Mo believe he will make it happen.

A basically self-educated man, Mo left college in 1967 after only three months, "bored to tears. I had a lot I wanted to do with my life, and school was just too slow," he says with a boyish grin. But if his formal education did not prepare him for success, his·years as a child on a thirteen-acre ranch in Palmer Lake, a tiny Colorado mountain town, did instill in him the love of nature on which his rapidly growing company rests. And from the age of seven, Mo has worked hard at anything he could find, with a perseverance handed down from his hardworking father, a successful businessman.

When Mo left college in 1967, he was partly motivated by a love of travel which is just as strong today. And as he explains, "that was during the Vietnam period. Young people made rather . . . harsh decisions then that they would not make today."

Before he turned nineteen Mo had started his first business: a health-food store in Aspen. "I made a living, that's all," he says, shrugging. But his interest in health grew, and he began to study herbs. Meanwhile he earned enough money to live on by painting houses, and then by demonstrating carrot juicers in health-food stores wherever he traveled. The slender, enthusiastic young man drew small audiences and began to become successful. "I loved it," he recalls. "I'd stick pineapples, watermelons, all sorts of good things through my carrot juicer."

But despite his success and his enjoyment of the work, Mo spent most of his time on a hobby. The whole subject of herbs, the thousands of years of folklore and the medicinal uses, fascinated him. He devoured every book he could find, went out in the field with naturalists, and collected herbs in the Rockies to blend teas for himself and his friends. Before long his entrepreneurial instinct surfaced and he was leading modestly priced nature walks into the mountains. "I was just so interested in herbs," he says, "I spent all my time working on them, studying them, thinking about them."

Herbs became a business for Mo via a classical route: as he served his blended teas to friends, they told him again and again, "Boy this is fantastic. You ought to sell it."

As a frequenter of health-food stores, Mo knew that in 1970 herbal products were sold almost entirely for health purposes; the general public did not see herb teas as something to drink for enjoyment. He also knew that herb teas were a staple of the European diet. But while several U.S. manufacturers had been in the business for as long as fifty years, "Nobody was doing a decent job with it."

For Mo "doing a decent job" meant creating teas so good that people would buy them for the taste. His brown eyes sparkle as he recounts his thinking at that time. "I began to realize how great it would be if I could sell herbs through the back door, so to speak. Make the herb tea taste so good that people would drink it, and then they'd get the health benefits." His study and experimentation led Mo to combinations of herbs. "I just wouldn't have peppermint plain," he explains. "I'd stick some chamomile in with it, or a bit of hibiscus, or something else. At that time, nobody sold blends in this country except for medicinal purposes."

By 1971 Mo's two-year hobby had become an obsession. That summer he and his wife, Peggy, went on a two-week camping trip with another couple, Wyck Hay and Lucinda Ziesing. "Everywhere we went," Mo remembers, "I'd say, 'Pull over, I've got to pick some of those plants!' " Wyck, who was interested in health himself, became more and more intrigued by the strange botanicals Mo bagged up to take home. At the end of the trip the two men agreed to go into business.

It started as a cottage industry—in an actual cottage. Outside Mo and Peggy's small house in the mountains, the young people built racks to hold screen doors. All day they picked herbs by the sackful, and then spread them out to dry on the screens. In forty-five days they picked nineteen gunnysacks full of tea. When they had built a mixing bin and Mo had created the first batch of Mo's 36 Herb Tea, they took some down to the health-food store in Boulder. The manager's response was instant and enthusiastic: "We'll buy everything you can bring us."

That winter the herbal-tea business was temporarily at a standstill with all its stock sold, so Mo and Peggy decided to do some traveling in South America, hoping to go down the Amazon River. Mo had visions of earning money by teaching English to the natives. But within a month Peggy discovered she was pregnant, so the couple headed back to Boulder.

When they arrived in early spring of 1971, they discovered that the health-food store had sold Mo's 36 Herb Tea all over the state. The name was well on its way to being famous. Mo winces at the recollection. "That was not exactly my favorite flavor. We picked too much wild oregano that year, and I personally thought it had a bitter aftertaste—a terpene taste. But they loved it. I don't think it would sell well today, but back then it went over big."

Despite the success of the tea, Mo could not afford to make a commitment to that business, not yet. Once again he sold carrot juicers and found odd jobs. Then John Hay, Wyck's brother, came out from New York. The two became fast friends, and before long had agreed to go into business together. While herbal tea now seems the only logical choice, at the time they debated whether to start a dried-fruit farm in western Colorado. But since nobody really wanted to move that far, Mo finally said, "Why don't we start the tea company up again? Everybody likes the tea. Let's do it."

About this time Mo overheard Lucinda Ziesing say that her nickname in high school had been Celestial Seasonings ("because she was so darn good-looking," he explains). The instant he heard that name, Mo said, "That's what we're going to call our company."

Celestial Seasonings' first production facility was a tiny old milking barn which belonged to the father of a friend, Michael Dominick. Michael, who volunteered the use of the barn, is today a shareholder of the company as well as one of its attorneys. For collateral the young entrepreneurs initially had eight hundred dollars realized from the sale of John Hay's car. Several months later, the company borrowed five thousand dollars from a local bank—but only when John's mother agreed to co-sign the loan.

Once again the young people picked herbs all day long, drying them on the screens. Since the loose tea had to be packaged somehow, they decided to make muslin bags—ten thousand of them. "Poor Peggy," Mo says, shaking his head. "I'd come home from picking herbs all day and there she was, pregnant and sewing those darn bags. It seemed like it took forever to do them. It was a huge job." But the muslin bags could be made with almost no capital investment. Old wire from the Bell System was purchased as an equally economical tie; the wire sheafing contained multicolored twine, which the women pulled out and clipped into short lengths to tie the bags.

Although everybody worked day and night, seven days a week, in the fall Mo had to take a job doing construction work to earn enough money to keep the business afloat. "We were *poor*," he says emphatically. "We were at the bottom of the poverty level. We had zero, zero, zero!"

Once they had traveling money, Mo and Peggy began a cross-country drive to New York, stopping at every health-food store along the way. In each town, Mo would consult the Yellow Pages to locate the stores and then drive over to make his pitch. "Good morning, this is our product. We're a brand-new company, Celestial Seasonings, and we will be the largest herb-tea company in the United States within three years."

"Sure, kid," they'd respond.

But the handpicked tea in the handmade bags sold. Even the very first packaging had a distinctive quality that would later become the hallmark of Celestial Seasonings: a paper inserted in each bag showed a picture of rabbits drinking tea. "From the mountains to the treetops, from the flowered valleys . . . we picked these herbs fresh for you," the paper said. The bag itself was identified with printing in meat-packing ink. Mo laughs now at the recollection. "I was such a health fanatic at that point that I insisted we take every precaution to make our product the healthiest ever. I figured if they could stamp that ink on meat, it would be safe to stamp it on the outside of the package. The *outside*, mind you.

"Well, I didn't realize it then, but if that ink got any water on it at all, it ran. One day I was giving my sales presentation in a health-food store in Chicago, 'This is Mo's 24 Herb Tea, and next we're coming out with Red Zinger,' when I noticed a strange look on the guy's face. He had picked up the bag to look at it, and the label had imprinted on his hands! His hands were sweaty, and that was all it took for that ink to run." After that the young company decided to use printer's ink instead of meat-packing ink for the packaging.

Mo's enthusiasm was unimpaired by that incident, and the trip east generated numerous orders. Today his enthusiasm is still so contagious that it is easy to imagine how effective the twenty-year-old entrepreneur was: "This is the best!" he would exclaim with full conviction. "We have the highest quality of anybody. You can't beat the health and nutrition, these herbs are so good for you. We picked them ourselves in the Colorado Rockies."

It was hard for anyone to turn him down.

As the winter of 1971 came on, the young people wondered how they would fill orders once their original stock was gone. Many of the herbs, once dried, were quickly used up in the teas. Red-clover blossoms, for instance, grew thick in a beautiful valley high in the mountains. Still, it took at least two hours of picking clover on hands and knees to pick enough to end up with a pound of dried clover. When Mo began investigating worldwide sources of herbs, he found that he could buy a pound of red-clover blossoms (at that time) for a dollar from Yugoslavia, and the blossoms were of equal quality. "What a surprise," he says ruefully.

Picking herbs, moreover, was not quite the same as sitting in the sun enjoying the flowers. Mo shakes his head and rubs his thick, reddish mustache. "People used to say to me, 'Mo, what a wonderful job you've got! How aesthetic!' And there I am, trudging up those canyons with 125 pounds of spearmint on my back. It was a lot of work, it's that simple. But that's okay. That's one of my theories: success requires work, work, work."

Although the days in the mountains picking herbs had been grueling, store owners were impressed by the fact that the herbs were handpicked. Moreover, for Mo the experience was personally valuable. "It was good for my life," he affirms. "Wonderful."

Celestial Seasonings' sales volume for 1971 was fifteen thousand dollars, not enough to cover expenses and pay the four young people enough to live on. But the response to Mo's 24 Herb Tea was encouraging; in March of 1972, the company incorporated. That year, the firm's first full year in business, sales went to seventy thousand. In 1973, sales doubled, and then doubled again in 1974 to reach $293,000.

In 1975, sales leaped almost 400 percent to over $1.3 million —but the company lost $4,000 that year. "We should have made some decent profit," Mo explains, "but we almost went broke because we tried to harvest peppermint in upper Wisconsin." With his extensive knowledge of herbs, Mo knew that peppermint grown in that region was the finest in the world. The company bought thirty-five standing acres, but lacked the technology to harvest and dry the mint. The plan was to sun-dry the mint in the field. "But the sun never came out," Mo says. "It rained and rained and rained. We built big drying bins, we tried everything, and nothing worked. Then a frost hit and we lost one-third of our crop overnight."

A fervent believer in self-education, Mo determined to learn from the experience. In 1975, the company bought a peppermint crop in another state where, as Mo affirms with an impish smile, "There was more sunshine," and harvested the first major peppermint crop in American history. Knowing that dealing with crops was always a gamble, Mo decided to play the percentages. As he says, "If you're going to win, you've got to take chances. You've just got to gamble wisely."

During the company's early years, Mo and his partner John Hay drew little money from Celestial Seasonings. In 1974, for instance, with sales at almost $300,000, Mo drew his largest annual salary from the company to date—$8,000. That year saw a relatively lavish personal investment, though: a washing machine shared by the Hay and Siegel families.

For all his belief in Celestial Seasonings, Mo sometimes wondered whether the hard work and doing without were worth it. During the first years he never knew whether there would be enough money to meet the payroll at the end of the week. Then, too, the ambitious young entrepreneur was haunted by his dream of someday heading a large company. "I wondered if I would learn more working for a big corporation. I was concerned about my personal development." The partners also had to fight the frustration they experienced whenever they approached a banker for a loan. "They thought the business was ridiculous," Mo says with a shrug. "They couldn't see how herb tea would ever sell in this country. But I *knew* it would because I saw how well it went over in Europe."

In the straitlaced, pin-striped world of bankers, Mo undoubtedly came across as a hippie, for all his growing expertise in business. Even today, media references to Celestial Seasonings often describe it as a company started by "a bunch of young hippies." It is an image that makes good copy, but does not quite describe the serious young people. Mo, who disagrees with the description, nevertheless accepts it with a broad grin: "My attitudes about life were definitely more punchy than they are today." With his long hair, his interest in natural health, and his outspoken views ons Vietnam, Mo Siegel undoubtedly did look like a member of the dropout generation. Today, however, his interest in health is shared by the majority of Americans; and his devotion to his work was always distinctly nonhippie.

Today Mo is still not easily categorized. His auburn hair and mustache are cut conservatively and kept neatly trimmed, but his dress varies wildly. For a meeting with conservative outsiders he may drive to work in a pin-striped suit, like a typical executive. On a warmer day, when no outside appointments are scheduled, he may don jeans or shorts and get on his bicycle. During the four-mile bike ride from home to office, however, Mo will not only be enjoying the scenery and building his aerobic health, but also listening to self-help tapes on his headphones, or perhaps to his tapes of Carl Sandburg on Lincoln. The bicycle is equipped with three packs, he points out, so that carrying work to and from the office never keeps him from biking.

The company itself is headquartered in an industrial park on the outskirts of Boulder, its third location. The 140,000 square feet used by Celestial Seasonings is spread among several buildings in the park, and represents quite an increase over the space in the previous location.

In 1972, when the company outgrew its milking barn, Mo found space for rent in a 6,400-square-foot building. A baker wanted the other half of the building. The problem was that the owner would not take Mo's signature on a lease. "Herb tea will never make it," he stated flatly. "You guys won't be around long enough to pay the rent."

The baker agreed to lease all the space and sublease to Celestial Seasonings.

"As fate would have it," says Mo, "the baker went under!" Some years later Mo ran into the ex-landlord who told him, "Mo, over the years I've really misjudged a couple of things, and your company was one of them."

Errors in judgment don't faze Mo, who believes that if you don't make mistakes it's because you never try anything. For his own ventures he uses a risk-ratio factor, a formula he developed to determine whether or not he should take a chance on a new idea. "Herb tea got a ninety-five-percent chance," he says, "so I knew it would succeed. Anything lower than eighty percent I won't even touch. I do every conceivable study on a project, I put my own intuition into it, and I come up with the factor." In 1979 Mo broke his own rule by giving the go-ahead to an undertaking other company executives were enthusiastic about, a new product called Salad Snacks. "Didn't work," he says matter-of-factly. "I knew it wasn't going to work, it had a risk-ratio factor below eighty percent. It's just a perfect example of what can happen when you break your own rules."

A person who makes his own rules, Mo will generally go ahead with his decisions no matter who disagrees with him. With a broad gesture he says, "Once I do my homework and my confidence level is high, I don't care if the whole world tells me I'm wrong, I'll go ahead. I don't care what it is. Sure, I'll fail. I've failed plenty of times. But I guess the key is how willing you are to stick with an idea and hammer away at it. No matter how grim things get, you've got to be persistent. When we first started this company I was poor, and for the next couple of years I stayed poor, but I knew it had to succeed if I just kept working. I had a vision, and it just had to come to be."

The company itself is one shining example of Mo's dogged persistence; another is the Red Zinger Bicycle Classic, which the company began sponsoring in 1975. There had never been a major bicycle race in the United States, and numerous people told Mo, "You can't introduce a new sport to this country, it just won't work."

"But I *knew* it would work," Mo says. "Bicycling was the second-largest sport in Europe. I saw half a million people waiting at the finish line of the Tour de France, a twenty-five-day race. I knew this sport could be popular in America, it just had to be presented properly."

Celestial Seasonings' presentation of the Red Zinger was so thorough that the first race claimed the attention of almost everyone in the company for six weeks. But the trick to creating the largest bicycle race in the country, Mo figured, was to pay the largest prize money and attract the top riders. The eight-day race has done that consistently, year after year, attracting over a hundred thousand fans and onlookers along the route through Boulder, Denver, Estes Park, Vail, and Colorado Springs. An established phenomenon, the race became an expensive piece of philanthropy for Celestial Seasonings, costing around $175,000 each year. Finally, after five years, with the race well established, Coors beer became the new sponsor. Mo is now happily exploring other ways the company can philanthropically promote American good health.

Why did the company promote a bicycle race? "It was a natural," Mo explains. "My whole life has been dedicated to good health. I believe in aerobic health, and nothing is better for the heart and lungs than bicycling. And since I like nature, I like to see the air around us clean, too." In 1974 when the race was founded, Mo and other Americans were concerned about the Arab oil blockade. Bicycling was an obvious alternative means of transportation. In short, Mo felt, "it would be good for America if people got into using the bicycle."

Mo says with a cheerful smile, "I've often thought I wasn't as much a businessman as a philosopher. But I've come to grips with my life; I know I'm a businessman. Of course, there's no reason a businessman can't be a philosopher."

Mo's philosophy has paid off handsomely for Celestial Seasonings. Nowhere is this more apparent than in the public response to the packaging of the now-famous teas. While packaging is an obvious marketing tool, Mo flatly denies that sales is the primary reason for the development of the artful, philosophic boxes Celestial Seasonings teas come in. "The space is there," he says. "Why not use it to do some good?"

From the beginning, the company had a commitment to the colorful fantasy that graces each box. John Hay's wife, Beth, did the first such picture, which still graces the box of Sleepytime Tea. "I wanted pretty pictures," Mo explains. For the pretty pictures, the company is willing to pay handsomely, hiring the best artists in this vein in the world. The painting in Mo's office of the emperor from Emperor's Choice Tea cost eight thousand dollars, for instance. The art on the boxes is probably best described as a combination of Norman Rockwell and Walt Disney, one of Mo's heroes. A typical example, the Red Zinger box, is brilliant red with yellow lettering. The circular picture on top and the rectangular picture which covers one side feature a white teacup with the red tea (which takes its color from hibiscus flowers) being struck by bolts of lightning—perhaps the "bolt of citrus flavor" mentioned on the package.

But as eye-appealing as the Celestial Seasonings artwork is, the words of wisdom on every available inch of the package represent the real triumph of Mo Siegel's philosophy. "As I said," he comments, "the space is there. If you can use the space to enrich other people's lives, then I say, 'By all means, do so.' "

Why not use the space to advertise the product? "People have advertising crammed down their throats all the time. If our packages can give them something about life, or something interesting, or something funny—then let's do it. But let's give them something that adds *human value*."

The sayings on the sides, bottom, and inside flaps of the package range from the humor of Mo Siegel ("Gravity has a lot of pull") to the wisdom of Confucius ("The man who in the view of gain thinks of righteousness; who in the view of danger is prepared to give up his life; and who does not forget an old agreement however far back it extends—such a man may be reckoned a complete man"). Each package invites tea drinkers to send in their ideas. As a result, the sayings on the packages are as diverse as the accumulated interests of Mo Siegel and the millions of fans of Celestial Seasonings teas.

A package usually includes something witty, such as this from Jonathan Ketchum, found currently on the Red Zinger package: "Voltaire is known for having said, 'If God had not existed, it would have been necessary to invent him.' However, if Voltaire had not existed, it would *not* have been necessary to invent him!" On the same package is another erxpression of Mo Siegel's philosophy, which he frequently quotes: "The most important thing a father can do for his children is to love their mother."

Cinnamon Rose, a softly romantic package, includes this: "Let your love be like the misty rain, coming softly but flooding the river." Country Apple, which comes with a nostalgic painting of apples, quotes Sophia Loren: "The world has lost its taste for simple things like the love of a woman for only one man."

Unquestionably the unique packages create instant product

identification and build loyalty among herb-tea drinkers. Also unquestionably, the packages are like they are because Mo simply wants to do something good with his life, "something good for other people." He pauses and looks out his window at the Rocky Mountains in the background. In part, he explains, he is driven by a persistent image of being called to judgment "when I've died and I'm resurrected on what I call the matching worlds. I imagine the Ancient of Days pulling out the record book and asking me, 'Mo, what did you do with your life?'

"Then I answer, 'Well, I sold more herb tea than anyone in the world.'

" 'Yeah, well what did you do with your life *that's of value?*'

" 'I cornered the soybean market; it was incredible, I made so much money.'

" 'But, Mo, *what did you do of value with your life?*'

"I think of that at least once a week. I want to make sure that when they open the record book I can say, 'I raised a good family. I put out products that were nutritionally good for people. I felt like I was serving people.' "

Mo's deep faith in God is that of a "nonkosher religionist," as he calls himself. The son of a Protestant mother and Jewish father, Mo attended a Catholic monastery school, where he faithfully hid in the basement during Mass. Although he does not attend church today, he considers his "friendship with God and my love for Him" the vital element in his life. Gesturing at a portrait on his office wall of another hero, Abe Lincoln, Mo says, "He didn't go to church either, and he was supposed to be the most religious president we ever had. Some of us just don't do well in the church environment."

Although Mo's religious beliefs are part of everything he does, he makes a firm attempt not to impose his beliefs on anyone. And while the packages often give philosophic or spiritual views, Mo avoids all directly religious overtones. "What I do," he says intensely, "I try to *be* the kind of person that I feel is right.

"That's not always easy. There's a story I heard from an old Indian in Oklahoma. He said, 'There's a great battle that rages inside me. It is represented by two sides.

" 'One side is the soaring eagle. Everything the eagle stands for is good and true and beautiful, and it soars above the clouds. Even though it dips down into the valleys, it's smart enough to lay its eggs on the mountaintops.

" 'The other side of me is represented by the howling wolf. And that raging, howling wolf represents the worst that's inside me. He eats upon my downfalls and justifies himself by his presence in the pack.'

"At that point," Mo continues, "the Indian stopped and an onlooker asked, 'Who wins this great battle?'

"And the wise old Indian replied, 'The one I feed.' "

Mo's strong identification with the eagle is seen in his endless self-education—he devours reading material and tapes—and in his commitment to high-flying goals. From the very beginning of the company, it has been his ambition to build a large corporation. Those who thought that at age twenty-one he was just dreaming are now taking him more seriously. And if anything, Mo's determination is strengthened by opposition.

"When people suggest that I'll never accomplish my goals," he says, "I just get more obstinate. I like to walk where people don't think I can. I don't just dream and watch to see if it'll happen; I work. You've got to work and plan and develop so you get the results you want. It's like in the early days in the business when I'd get resistance from retailers. They'd say, 'Why do we want your herb tea on the shelves when we've already got this other one? We only want one.' Sorry, but if I heard that, I was going to come back and back and back. Nothing would stop me, not even if I had to call back sixteen times until I got the job done."

Today Celestial Seasonings is handled by approximately three hundred distributors and sold through an estimated twenty-five thousand retail outlets, including many large supermarkets. Because of the company's phenomenal success, giant food companies such as Lipton and Tetley have begun to enter the herb-tea business. Mo's attitude toward this is typically positive. "The more customers their advertising converts to herb tea, the better off we'll be. Those companies will train people to buy our products."

Mo's optimism and perseverance are matched by his desire to

do a good job—in fact, a very good job, although he insists, "I don't want to be a nut for perfection. Only God can achieve that." Mo enjoys pointing out that Walt Disney was another near-perfectionist. "He always insisted that you should do the best you can. And if you do, the public will respond. Look at what Disney did with *Snow White*. He had a million celluloid drawings that he wasn't satisfied with, so he stuck them in the trash can. It cost him a fortune, but he was a *nut* for doing it right."

Disney's work is the standard Mo holds out for Celestial Seasonings' packaging. His frequent memos to marketing people stress that every piece of art should be something Disney would applaud. "Or don't bring it to my office," the memos conclude. "I don't want to see it."

In reaching for excellence, Mo has methodically surrounded himself with a top-notch management team, including a former executive at Coca-Cola, a former vice-president at Pepsi, the former head engineer for Pepperidge Farms, and a former manager at General Foods. Other key people also have experience at major corporations, including Lipton, Quaker Oats, General Mills, and Norton Simon. The staff of the research laboratory—where several scientists now spend endless hours studying herbs, as Mo once did—includes a Ph.D. "As somebody once said," Mo explains, " 'Never hire anybody unless they're smarter than you.' That's not too difficult for me."

While Celestial Seasonings offers competitive salaries to new employees, one of the key features in attracting high-quality people has been the stock-option plans Mo makes available. Mo believes in this kind of "sharing," both philosophically and as a businessman. "I've already made a lot of money, and how much can I spend? It makes me very happy to see people come into this company and do well, grow, and reap financial benefit. They're working hard and they deserve part of it. If American business would do more along these lines, we'd see higher productivity and a rise in the GNP. It would do wonders for the attitude toward work, for quality control, and for the standard of excellence. When people own part of the company, they're going to perform." The Celestial Seasonings Employee Stock Ownership Plan is now the second-largest shareholder in the company.

The same interest in international business that led Mo to believe in 1971 that herb tea would sell in the United States has led him to study Japanese methods of motivating employees. He has also extensively studied the practices of IBM (Thomas Watson, IBM's founder, is yet another of Mo's heroes). As a result, this year Celestial Seasonings is installing a gain-sharing plan that will incorporate the use of work teams. "I like to see the person on the machine put his brains into how to make things work better," Mo says. His present vision is of work teams which will spend one paid hour a week examining production problems and thinking up solutions. Mo explains, "If you tell them, 'Hey, we're having a problem with the paint chipping,' they'll usually say, 'Thanks for asking us. You see, the problem is that every time the part goes through this particular machine, it rubs. . . .' "

Already in operation at Celestial Seasonings are quarterly group meetings in which a cross section of company managers discuss individual goals along with company goals and objectives. Mo's expectations of his management are as high as his expectations of himself. "Look," he says, "if the company grew thirty-five percent last year, how much did you grow? If you grew less than thirty-five percent, you're destined for trouble at Celestial Seasonings. Even inflation grows at fifteen percent; anyone can at least grow at twice that speed!"

Mo's populist approach has not always had the results he desired. Once, when the company had imported a supply of rooibos from South Africa, employees objected so strenuously to trade with that country that the herb had to be eliminated from the product line.

Good people are attracted to Celestial Seasonings not just by stock options and salaries, but by the relaxed work atmosphere. The informal dress—one executive may wear shorts and a sweatshirt while another is in suit and tie—is a symbol of the free and easy management style. "We only expect two things out of people that work here," says Mo. "We want you to be nice and do a good job. That's all. If you've got those two qualities, you can win at Celestial Seasonings."

But perhaps the most attractive feature Celestial Seasoning offers employees is its remarkable growth. During the past five years the company's average annual rate of growth has been 40 percent. Mo's goal for annual sales, presently at seventeen million dollars, is fifty million by 1986. "When you demonstrate your ability to grow," he stresses, "you can attract good people and keep them. If a company doesn't grow, it loses its ability to motivate people, because without growth there is no opportunity for advancement. But when people see growth, they know there will be something for them to share in."

For Celestial Seasonings, growth has also entailed growing pains. When the company hit the five-million-dollar mark, Mo became deeply involved in planning, and brought in General Electric models to illustrate what he wanted to do with Celestial Seasonings. "When you've got a little ma and pa company," he says with a grimace, "and you try to grow, there are those who don't want to. There were some people who strongly protested what I was doing. 'What is this stuff?' they asked. 'What are you doing to this company?' I had to push some of them out the door because they resisted growth. I used to go home at night and say, 'Peggy, I can't take this another day. It's awful. My friends —I'm making them leave.' " Today, although several of the original people at Celestial Seasonings remain stockholders, Mo is the only one still actively involved in the management of the business.

Mo remains committed to building a company structure capable of supporting long-range growth. "We're doing seventeen million dollars in sales right now," he says, "but when I hire people, they're people capable of running a hundred-million-dollar business. So they can be around for a long time."

When Mo refers to a hundred-million-dollar business by 1988, he means it. Every decision made at Celestial Seasonings is made with reference to this goal; typically, Mo isn't just dreaming—he's working. In planning for growth, he is interested not only in people and corporate structure, but in diversification of the product line. Although today Celestial Seasonings' fame rests on Grandma's Tummy Mint, Iced Delight, Mandarin Orange, and other blended herbal teas, to Mo it is "not an herb-tea company, but a health company." In the near future other kinds of health products will be added to the company's present line of over forty teas. Meanwhile, more than five hundred million cups and glasses of Celestial Seasonings tea will contribute to the national health this year.

"Sure, I like money," Mo says. "It's green, warm, and it pays the rent. But money is not my number-one motivator. I like good health."

In 1979 Mo took a group of gerontologists, doctors, and other health experts to the Soviet Union to observe "the long-dwellers"—mountain people who are reputed to live more than a hundred years. His friendly brown eyes light up when he talks about the trip. "It was fabulous. The idea of people living to the age of one hundred, and living *well*—healthy, intelligent, vibrant —that can happen in this country, too. And I believe it will. When it does, and I feel I can contribute to that cause, then I'm going to be happy with what I have done."

For Mo, an interest in extending life is natural. "When I look at the stars and think how vast and dynamic the universe is," he says, "I realize I don't know *anything*. I want to learn. I figure maybe by the time I'm sixty or sixty-five, I'll begin to tap my ability. I don't look at myself slowing down for a long time. I envision myself being a very old man, and still going for it every day!"

Conclusion

Many readers of this book have probably found themselves asking, *"Why didn't I think of that first?"* The truth is that a great many things look far easier after the fact than they did in the beginning. I'm reminded of a horrendous afternoon I once spent putting together a backyard jungle gym for my children. It took me nearly six hours—but once it was assembled, I could have set up a second one in thirty minutes.

Most people are probably fortunate that they *didn't* think of these ideas first. If they had, they might very well have failed miserably. The odds against succeeding with any of these ideas were undoubtedly very high; in fact, the odds aren't very good for *any* new enterprise, and the more offbeat the concept, the less chance it has of succeeding. The individuals who made these concepts work are just as unusual as the concepts themselves. Indeed, it takes a very unusual person to make ideas like these work.

What are some of the personal qualities that enabled the entrepreneurs in this book to do what they did?

Perhaps tenacity is the most obvious characteristic they share. In almost every case, numerous people issued sincere warnings that the new venture was doomed to fail. Imagine how often Gary Dahl was told, "You've got rocks in your head!" when he talked about selling a rock with a training manual. Dave Schwartz heard the same thing: "What, are you crazy? Who would rent an old car?" Art Dore was asked, "Who would pay to see rank amateurs box? Nobody, that's who. It's hard enough to make money promoting professional fights!" Xavier Roberts' critics wondered who would ever spend two hundred dollars on a baby doll (excuse me, a Little Person). As you can see, uncertain people would never go ahead with projects like these. Unusual ideas can be developed only by strong-willed individuals who are blind to the possibility of failure.

The people in this book have other common denominators characteristic of successful people in any field. They work hard; they manage their time well; they're disciplined and extremely motivated; and they enjoy their work immensely. They are also exciting, creative people whose enthusiasm is contagious. Often that enthusiasm was an important factor in promoting the product or service, as well as in convincing others to join the business in the early stages.

If you're going to start a unique business, being young and reckless apparently helps. Every one of these ventures was founded by a man or woman under forty. Five of them—Slinky, Wham-O, BabyLand General, Rent-a-Wreck, and Celestial Seasonings—were started by entrepreneurs in their early twenties. Mo Siegel, in fact, was only nineteen when he opened a health-food store in Aspen—a business which was the seed for the herbal-tea company he founded shortly thereafter.

Starting businesses like these seems to require more spunk and persistence than money. Celestial Seasonings was initially capitalized with only eight hundred dollars, money realized from the sale of an automobile; not until several months later was five thousand dollars borrowed from a local bank. Seven dollars down and seven dollars a month bought the band saw which cut the first Wham-O products—and started one of the world's leading toy companies on its way. Richard and Betty James manufactured only four hundred Slinkies originally; on a paycheck of fifty dollars a week, that was all they could afford. To capitalize Eastern Onion, Mary Flatt had to sell her car for seven hundred dollars and borrow another five hundred dollars from an old high school girl friend. Like Mary, Xavier Roberts used a car (in fact, two cars) as collateral for a loan when he borrowed five thousand dollars to start BabyLand General.

Only two of the ten entrepreneurs in this book had access to significant amounts of capital when they began. Marvin Wernick, who first manufactured the Mood Ring, was already established in the jewelry business at that time. Art Dore was a self-made millionaire when he conceived of the Toughman Contest. (It's worth remembering, however, that he made his money in demolition—a business he started with only a crowbar and a sledgehammer!)

While some of these ideas, like the Pet Rock and the Slinky, were brand-new, others were new slants on established products and services. Rent-A-Wreck, for instance, is a sensible variation on the new-car rental business. BabyLand General's Little People are either different baby dolls or cleverly marketed soft sculptures, depending on your point of view. Eastern Onion grew out of Mary Flatt's observation of a traditional Western Union singing telegram. And amateur boxing had been around for a long time when Art Dore put a new and different slant on it.

These very successful entrepreneurs are characterized by their ability to take existing products or concepts and present them in new and exciting ways. Marvin Wernick, for instance, did not invent liquid crystals, but he was the first to see how they could be used in the jewelry industry. Karen Dwyer and Patrika Brown certainly didn't invent either fine baked goods or erotica, but they did combine the two to create a new concept: the Erotic Baker. When Mo Siegel began blending herbs for teas, he was reviving a very ancient skill; his exciting marketing concepts are undoubtedly responsible for a large part of Celestial Seasonings' success.

As these stories show, distribution is vital to the success of a new product; most of the people in this book had to learn how to distribute their products. Many of the products—the Hula Hoop, the Pet Rock, the Slinky, the Frisbee, the Superball, the Mood Ring, the Little People, and Celestial Seasonings' herb teas—were retailed through third parties. It is often the case with such products that a middleman must approach the retailer with the products. Knowing this, both Xavier Roberts and the Jameses spent considerable time and effort at various gift and toy shows lining up good manufacturers' representatives. Marvin Wernick's success was largely due to his excellent distribution of his product when the Mood Ring fad hit.

Entrepreneurs must be good at every phase of handling a small business, and especially at generating free publicity, since they often cannot afford to buy advertising. Every one of the people in this book has been written up in national magazines and newspapers, and has appeared on national television. Often, free major publicity can make a new product or service successful overnight. When *Newsweek* did half a page on the Pet Rock, "the whole thing exploded," as Gary Dahl says. Gary was immediately contacted by hundreds of magazines, newspapers, and radio and television stations from all over America. He appeared on such national shows as *The Tonight Show* and *Tomorrow* in a publicity blitz that would have cost millions of dollars—except that no amount of money can buy publicity like that. In Gary's case, his expertise in public relations was no doubt a factor in helping generate the publicity that turned the Pet Rock into an American phenomenon.

Many other ideas in this book have also caught the attention of the national press. The Erotic Baker has received considerable coverage in national magazines, including *Playboy*, *Money*, and *New Times*, and Rent-A-Wreck has been featured in *Newsweek*, *Time*, and numerous other national magazines, while founder Dave Schwartz has appeared to talk about his idea on almost every national television talk show. Art Dore's concept has created similar interest, and Art has appeared on *Phil Donahue*, *PM Magazine*, and *Real People*. Both Celestial Seasonings and BabyLand General have earned feature articles in *The Wall Street Journal* as well as other publications. So, while the unique nature of these concepts can create difficulties, the same uniqueness can also help gain invaluable publicity.

Perhaps the ability to generate free national publicity is to be expected of young entrepreneurs who are accustomed to thinking big. All of the people in this book are not only positive thinkers, they are individuals who like to do things in a big way. Even at the beginning, when their businesses were only dreams, they felt this. Mo Siegel's presentation to prospective retailers is a good example: "We're a brand-new company, Celestial Seasonings, and we will be the largest herb-tea company in the United States within three years."

Art Dore also thought big when he put together the First Annual U.S. and Canadian Championship Toughman Contest—with a first-prize purse of fifty thousand dollars. "Nobody believed it," Art says. "Nobody believed I was going to go out and pick out a bunch of guys off the street and let them fight, and then give fifty thousand dollars to the winner!" But he did, and he drew a gate of fourteen thousand people.

Xavier Roberts is another man who has always thought big, and still does. BabyLand General "will be a billion-dollar-plus business someday," he says confidently. And then, expressing the philosophy of many successful entrepreneurs, he adds, "If you ever want to do anything big, first you've got to think big."

When a product is very unusual, it is sometimes destined to be a fad item, with enormous overnight success and a rapid decline in popularity. It may be that no businessman is ever quite prepared for the huge demand that sometimes occurs for a new item. As Gary Dahl's story shows, when an item does become a fad, the entrepreneur must be prepared to work day and night seeing to it that orders are filled. Moreover, Marvin Wernick advises that a manufacturer is fortunate if he is not caught with a huge overstock when the item loses momentum. Even when a fad item is not profitable (as in the case of the Hula Hoop on its first release), a businessperson can learn from the experience and go on to future success, as Spud Melin and Rich Knerr did—they made millions on their next product, the Frisbee.

Slinky and Frisbee have become household words, not only in America, but around the world. Why do these products enjoy such longevity while Mood Rings and Pet Rocks peak and fade out within a few months? Apparently the answer is in the product itself. Gary Dahl comments that the Pet Rock "died because it got to the point where everyone had heard the joke." Marvin Wernick believes this is true of any novelty item, such as the Mood Ring. "They just get tired of talking about it," he says. The Slinky, on the other hand, seems to have an enduring entertainment value for children. Like the Slinky, the Frisbee is visually interesting, helps develop motor skills, works without batteries, and most important, is an endless source of fun.

Eastern Onion, the Erotic Baker, Rent-A-Wreck, the Tough-man Contest, Celestial Seasonings, and BabyLand General have already survived longer than the typical fad product. Will their success continue to build? One positive indicator is that each business has been steadily expanding; several offer a diversified product line that keeps satisfied customers coming back for more —whether it's another Little Person, more Red Zinger tea, or an elegant new Frisbee. Since none of these six businesses is more than a few years old, it's too soon to predict which of them will become household words. But judging from their present success, it's a sure bet that at least some of them will become permanent features on the American scene.

I want to thank the people in this book for sharing their valuable time with me, so that I in turn could share these stories with you. All of us can be grateful to these people and the many others like them whose creativity and boldness give us something new from time to time. Their concepts make the world a little different, a little more fun—and a better place to live in.

ABOUT THE AUTHOR

ROBERT L. SHOOK is Chairman of the Board of the American Executive Corporation and contributing editor of *Success Unlimited* magazine. His bestselling books include *The Entrepreneurs*, *Ten Greatest Salespersons*, and *Winning Images*.

All About Business from the MENTOR Library

All About Business from MENTOR

From the MENTOR Executive Library

SIGNET and MENTOR Books of Special Interest

☐ **HOW TO FIND WORK by Jonathan Price.** The step-by-step guide to landing the job you want—whether you're just out of school or re-entering the work force. Includes 300 job descriptions and self-evaluation quizzes. (120701—$3.50)*

☐ **HOW TO GET A BETTER JOB QUICKER by Richard A. Payne. New expanded edition.** The remarkable step-by-step plan that has already helped thousands move up the ladder of success. "By far the best book on getting a new job"—*Industrial Engineering.*
(620941—$2.95)

☐ **YOU ARE WHAT YOU WEAR by William Thourlby.** A must for every man! Package yourself for success—in everything from business to sex—with this essential guide to choosing, buying, and wearing clothes to achieve every goal . . . "An excitingly different approach to the success look . . . intelligent and perceptive . . ."—*Athens Banner-Herald* With an 8-page photo insert of vital "dos" and "don'ts".
(121953—$2.95)*

☐ **THE NEW EXECUTIVE WOMAN: A Guide to Business Success by Marcille Gray Williams.** A total guide to overcoming the obstacles a woman faces in the buisness world, and to locating the strengths and strategies she needs to climb the corporate ladder.
(619331—$2.75)

Prices slightly higher in Canada